GRINDR SERIAL KILLER

STEPHEN PORT

KILLER QUEENS
BOOK THREE

ALAN R. WARREN

House of Mystery Publishing

Seattle, Washington, USA

Vancouver, British Columbia, Canada

First Edition

ISBN (Hardback): 978-1-989980-63-7
ISBN (Paperback): 978-1-989980-64-4
ISBN (eBook): 978-1-989980-62-0

Cover design, formatting, layout, and editing by Evening Sky Publishing Services

CONTENTS

PREFACE

Killer Queens is a new series of historical fiction books based on true stories. Sources, such as police reports and newspaper articles, are examined to gather as many facts surrounding each case. As with any work of fiction, some creative additions were made when recounting these stories, usually in the conversations between the personalities involved. The various sources are the basis of these conversations and, hopefully, make them come alive for the readers to help understand what was meant by those words.

One of the most common questions in gay-related murders is: how are they different from heterosexual murders? This question is important, as homosexuality was considered a criminal act for so many years. The *Killer Queens* series of books explores the world of murder in the gay community, whether the victims or the killers themselves, and sometimes both, are homosexual.

If you were caught performing a homosexual act in the Victorian Era, they would say you were "sexually insane" and commit you to an insane asylum. By the early 1900s, most countries decided it was more of a deviant act, something you shouldn't do. They would put you in a regular prison instead of an insane asylum if caught. By doing so, homosexuality became a crime, not as severe as murder, but more on the level of crimes such as theft, burglary, or arson.

A stunning example of the treatment of homosexuals in society is that of Alan Turing. Turing was a British mathematician, cryptanalyst, and computer scientist during World War II. In 1939, he joined the Hut 8 team. There, he solved the German Enigma code, which was considered the turning point for the Allied Forces winning the war against the Nazis.

So, what did society decide to do with one of its heroes?

Alan Turing was a homosexual. In 1952, when he was 39 years old, he started a relationship with Arnold Murray, who was 19. Shortly after the couple began seeing each other, Turing's house was robbed. After the police investigated the crime, they discovered that the thief was Murray and that Turing and Murray had been acquainted. It was also found that the two men had been involved in a sexual relationship. Both men were charged with gross indecency. Turing later pleaded guilty to the charges and was convicted. He was given a choice between imprisonment or conditional probation. What were the conditions he had to meet?

Turing had to undergo physical and hormonal changes designed to reduce his libido. He received several injections over one year, which feminized his body. During that year, he became impotent and grew breast tissue. Along with his body changes, he had his security clearance removed and lost his job with the British Intelligence Agency. He tried to move to America, but they denied him as he was then a convicted felon.

On June 7, 1954, Turing committed suicide in his home by ingesting cyanide. His housekeeper found him with a half-eaten apple lying beside him in his bed the following day. It was hypothesized that he had doused the apple with the cyanide. An inquest later determined that he had committed suicide.

When society forces one of its citizens to be sterilized for being homosexual, one considered to be among the best and a war hero, why would they care about other homosexuals being murdered or hurt?

It didn't end there.

Even after homosexuality was legalized in 1967, it was still considered a sickness or illness in the medical community that needed curing. Almost like alcoholism, only the general public looked at alcoholics with sympathy. After all, they were still pleasing people, and it was just the alcohol that made them do bad things. It was the Christian thing to do to help them. Most alcoholics weren't even arrested for driving while drunk or starting a fight in a public place. They were merely told to go home and sleep it off; if they kept on fighting, they were put in the drunk tank by the police for a night.

Whereas, if you were having or attempting to have sex with someone of the same sex as yourself, you were a pervert. It was considered wrong, disgusting, dirty, and perverted behavior. It was also judged as something you didn't need to do.

Why would someone want to have sex with another of their same-sex?

The public didn't know what to do with homosexuals after they were no longer considered criminals or insane. At least with alcoholics and drug addicts, there were treatments for their problems; after all, they just needed not to do it!

So, what would they do when they couldn't arrest these homosexuals or put them into the local mental institute? History repeated itself, and they turned it over to the religion of the day to handle.

In the past, when "dealing with" the Indigenous people of North America, the church and state decided that to "civilize the savage," they had their children forcibly extracted from the reserves they were imprisoned on and taken to Catholic schools to learn how to be "good Christians." Only now, many years later, an astounding number of unmarked graves are being discovered all over Canada, where Indigenous children were buried after their deaths at these residential schools. We do not even know the names of these children or why or how they died. Despite this atrocity, they believed they were successful in those cases with people they didn't understand, and they figured they would be successful in handling the gay population with the same iron fist.

So, keeping up with societal tradition, Evangelicals developed a new program to cure homosexuals. It was called "Exodus." In other words, they intended to "Pray away the Gay." They convinced several young gay men and women that the devil's influence made them believe they were gay and could fix their "problem" if they turned their lives over to the Lord and worked through the Exodus program. If they did, they would be cured, but they would be able to live healthy, productive, straight lives. As with so many other religious plans to remedy what didn't need healing, it left many young gays confused, in despair, and committing suicide.

A significant component of the books in this series will include an individual analysis of the killers. In some cases, the question of who the murderer was about will be examined – whether the murderer was about the person they desired or the person at the heart of the murder. From the killers' outlook, was their reason for committing murder different because of their sexual orientation? Or was the murder about the act of desiring them?

The answer to this question is entirely different when the victims are also gay. After all, like any other minority group or class of people in the world, being a minority creates a reason for some to want to kill them. The sexual component is complex, so it will take several examples to understand. Some cases involve both the killer and the victim being homosexual. In these particular cases, we can see quite a few similarities to that of heterosexual murderers. We will find emotional perspectives to be the major causes of the murders. The motive could be anything from jealousy to unreciprocated love or the actual murderer unable to find love due to mental issues or social circumstances. But most importantly, in all those cases, the type of love, albeit homosexual or heterosexual, is only the affections of such devotion.

The previous two books of this series explored the lives and murders of LGBTQ people in the early twentieth century. It was a time when not only was homosexuality considered a sickness that had to be cured and a crime that would send you to prison. Now, I jump to the future and more modern times in book three and into the new millennium. The last one hundred years have seen much progress within the western world. Not only is being gay no longer a crime or considered a mental illness, but in several countries, LGBTQ people are allowed to be legally married, and there is no longer a stigma attached to gays when it comes to murder.

This book is based on the case of Stephen Port, a serial murderer in London, U.K. Indeed, we should be able to assume that the murder investigation and the pursuit of Port were carried out with a great desire to stop the murders by capturing the culprit and handled professionally by law enforcement. Sadly, this was not what happened. Law enforcement showed a complete lack of caring or urgency in solving this case until after the fifth murder, when family members of one of the victims forced them to investigate by putting extreme pressure on them by going to the media.

One of the biggest problems the police demonstrated was a total lack of empathy for the victims. The police officers on duty automatically considered them as "just" gay prostitutes and drug addicts after their bodies were discovered in a city park. They unjustly attributed the deaths of these young men to drug overdoses even when there was obvious evidence showing them something different.

Along with the lack of interest in this case by police, law enforcement had to develop a new type of detection centered around the internet. The recent explosion in social media, which involved almost every aspect of younger people's lives for meeting and connecting with others, was all brand new. It was a whole new world where people could find other people to have sex with a simple click on their phones while using an app. They no longer had to write ads and place them in newspapers where they would eventually get an answer asking to meet for a date or spend all night at a loud smokey nightclub. Not only was it easier than ever before, but it was instant.

On top of being a speedy way to meet up with someone, there was a certain sense of privacy. You couldn't be seen going into a bar or leaving some meeting place with a date. But with this privacy, there was no protection if the date went terribly wrong since nobody knew who you had met.

Meeting up with someone through an internet website or app isn't any more dangerous than through a nightclub or newspaper advertisement within its method. But it's primarily more hazardous because it's much harder to find where and with whom you went. Anybody can sign up online under a fake name and even picture, and you wouldn't know it until you meet them. It makes it more difficult to trace because when you walk into a nightclub, there are many witnesses and possibly even cameras, or when you place an ad in the newspaper, you would have to give your real name and pay for the ad with your credit card. It makes for a more accessible investigation for the police. The police could also go back through the newspapers to find the phone number or address the person wanted to be contacted.

INTRODUCTION

On Thursday, October 15, 2015, the London Metropolitan Police came to Stephen Port's one-bedroom flat on Cooke Street in Barking, East London. It was a crisp cloudy Fall day to place Port into custody and charge him with the murders of four men. Other charges included six counts of administering poison, seven charges of rape, and four charges of sexual assault. Later, while Port was in custody, the prosecutors added another eight counts of poisoning in July of 2016 for a total of twenty-nine charges against him.

When Stephen Port was arrested, he was placed into the Level an HMP (Her Majesty's Prison) Belmarsh, the highest security prison category, based on the severity of the crime and the risk posed if the prisoner escaped. The prison is adjacent to the Woolwich Crown Court in southeast London, where high-profile cases are often heard. The Belmarsh Prison was also used to house all people who posed a threat to the country's National Security—quite a few of them were detained indefinitely without charge under the Crime and Security Act of 2001.

According to a May 17, 2016 report by *The Daily Mail* in the U.K., a former inmate claimed that the Belmarsh maximum security jail is like "a jihadist training camp, where extremists brainwash young prisoners to spread the terror message across the whole prison system." In this report, 28 inmates were being held for terrorism-related offenses. A group of jihadists who call themselves "The Akhi" (Arabic for brother) appear to be almost running the prison. This environment creates a problem for the other inmates, especially young offenders like Stephen Port, who the Akhi try to indoctrinate and brainwash into their beliefs to create a more extensive network of terrorists. With his dissimilar sexuality to what is usually found in the Akhi, Port would not be accepted in such an extreme group, and his life could become threatened.

The atmosphere in the Belmarsh Prison left Stephen Port feeling very alone and quite vulnerable. His parents could not visit him, and he was in his cell for up to 23 hours daily. His only means of communication was to exchange letters with his family, friends, or anybody on the outside. This is how a man by the name of Cody Lachey came into Stephen's life to help fill the empty void that Stephen had been now living locked away in prison.

In the winter of 2015, Stephen received a letter in prison from someone he had never heard of before. It wasn't long before Stephen realized that being all over the news on television, radio, and the internet would put him in the spotlight— in prison, the U.K., and the world. Soon, he would start receiving letters from dozens of men and women looking to get to know him, often in a romantic way.

I met Cody Lachey after seeing him on *Crime and Investigation*, a U.K.-based television documentary. Cody had been on the program discussing several serial killers in Britain. He claimed to have known some of them and communicated with several of them. One was Stephen Port.

Cody Lachey is an ex-convict who had been in prison in the U.K. three times, once in the HMP Manchester, known as the notorious "Strangeways," and twice in Salford's Forest Bank Prison. The 35-year-old, 6' 4" tall man had been shot at and stabbed several times before serving his time in prison. Cody had been involved in the criminal underworld and was a drug dealer, but he is now reformed and living in Manchester, England. He has become a crime commentator, covering all aspects of his personal history, including living a life of crime and being in prison. He has been on several documentaries, spoken to criminology students, and given in-depth perspectives on prison reform in the U.K.

Cody told me,

> It was from my childhood where I was raised watching serial killer and gangster documentaries that I went on to be involved with all of the lifestyles. My early lifestyle is also what started me writing to serial killers who were in prison. I enjoyed discussing the cases with the killers and wanted to hear their sides of the story. I first wrote to Stephen Port after he was charged with the four murders and a whole host of other offenses. I read a news article stating that Port was in the HMP Belmarsh, and I knew how to write to prisoners from being in prison myself earlier. So, I wrote to him, and he replied. We went from there.
>
> We corresponded for months, and I couldn't believe how open he was

discussing his case with me from the very first letter. As a former prisoner myself, it was obvious that he wasn't clued up that he was on remand, and it was well known that if you're in prison on remand, you don't discuss your case with anyone, whether that be speaking on the phone or in letters. Even with your cellmate, you say nothing, as anything you say or do can be used as evidence against you, but Port was very much an open book."

I have included many of these letters in Part IV of this book. Hopefully, they will give you, the reader, a great perspective on Stephen Port and how he thinks. Stephen described what happened on the nights of these crimes and offered his defense of the murders.

Did Stephen Port kill these men and possibly more? Or was he just an innocent man who got into a lifestyle of chemsex, and it was merely bad luck that at least four of his partners who participated in chemsex with him turned up dead?

As with many of my other crime books before this one, there is a question of how the police and courts dealt with the crimes. The status and circumstances of the victims were distinct. And even if law enforcement didn't care that each of the murder victims was gay, there is still a question of why law enforcement did nothing to investigate each of these crimes. As you read through the cases of these murder victims, you will see that there was absolutely no investigation completed. Even when the autopsies showed that there were genuine questions, the metro police just closed each case and ruled them overdoses.

Grindr Serial Killer is a story of a serial killer and how he was assisted by the unfortunate uncaring attitude of the metropolitan police, who ignored a mountain of evidence suggesting several murders of the gay community were happening in Barking. Because of their callous attitude, a serial killer was given free rein to do what he wanted, when he wanted, and even how he wanted to commit these murders.

Currently, the police are reassessing 58 unexplained deaths of homosexuals involving the date rape drug GHB between June 2011 and October 2015 to ensure foul play has not been missed. It should be mentioned that the churchyard at St. Margaret was known as a place for men to meet each other for quick, anonymous sexual encounters—one of the reasons the police never thought twice about a gay man being found dead from an overdose.

PART I

SERIAL KILLER STEPHEN PORT

1

BACKGROUND

Stephen John Port was born on February 22, 1975, in Southend-On-Sea, Britain. His parents moved to Dagenham about a year after he was born. Stephen spent most of his time alone and was very withdrawn at school. He didn't get along with the other students, which is probably why he didn't socialize with the other students much. His neighbors always considered Stephen a much older soul, almost like an adult, not a child.

Port had one sister, Sharon, two years older than him, and his parents, his father, Albert, who worked cleaning offices, and his mother, Joan, who worked as a supermarket cashier. His parents were not comfortable with Stephen's gay lifestyle, but they tolerated it. Albert blamed Stephen's lifestyle on the fact that he was shy and introverted. Albert also didn't like that his son would never listen to his advice, which he believed led to someone taking advantage of Stephen and turning him gay.

When Port turned 16, he wanted to attend an art college. But his parents couldn't afford it, so he went to a chef school for two years instead. He started working in local restaurants and cooked for weddings and other events. Later, he got a job with the West Ham Bus Depot and worked there for a few years to save enough money to get his apartment away from home.

In 2006, just after he came out to his friends and family, he moved into an apartment in the Barking area of London. Joan Port regularly visited him there, and she said that Stephen was immaculate and tidy, always keeping his apartment clean and orderly. Sharon, Stephen's sister, also stated that there was a man who always paid for Stephen's household bills regularly, but she had never met the man and didn't know who he was.

It wasn't long before Port started to enjoy his newfound freedom, where he would have large parties and several male partners over almost every night. His friends and coworkers soon complained about his changing behavior and Port becoming very selfish.

Port claimed to have worked as a Special

Needs Teacher at Westminster Kingsway College in King's Cross and as a former Seaman with the Royal Navy. His resume also claimed that he had graduated from the University of Oxford and was from Hornchurch in Barking, East London. Port had all this information on his Facebook page and said he had also worked as a chef and helped disabled students learn how to cook. Before that, it claimed that he was a door-to-door sales clerk.

Most of those claims were not true. Instead, Port worked as a male escort and started selling his body to men when he was about 30 years old. He charged 800 pounds per night or 100 pounds per 1-hour session. Port was very popular with his escort services and had several excellent reviews on The *Daily Mail*. He also became the drug supplier at several chemsex parties that became popular in the early 2000s. These parties soon became the center of all of his social activity.

Port did appear on one *Celebrity Master Chef UK* episode, the fourth episode of the season, in June 2014. In it, he cooked with the JLS singer JB Gill and soap opera star Emma Barton.

Over the first year of living alone, Port met several people who liked to Party and Play—a newer trend within the gay community in the early 2000s London, where several men would get together and take drugs that enhanced their sexual performance. Afterwhich, they engaged in sexual activity with everyone else in the room. In the community, it was called "Chemsex." Port became the drug supplier at several chemsex parties, and these parties soon became the center of his social activity. The most popular drugs used were methamphetamines such as crystal meth, Tina, or T. Some other drugs used were GHB, GBI, or

Stephen Port as a Chef

Mephedrone. These were quite often known as poppers. At the time, these drugs were all illegal in London.

Methamphetamines will delay the need for sleep, and on them, people could stay awake for days. They also heighten their sexual arousal and, at the same time, inhibit the ability of men to ejaculate. A person could take the drugs, keeping them high for about eight hours. This would allow men at these parties to have sex for hours. At some of these parties, the sexual activities could last for days. So, they would have to reuse the pills a couple of times per day.

Another distinguishing factor of these parties was how the people took their drugs. Several people were using needles, but most were also having unprotected sex. So, if you injected the drugs, it was called "slam sex." These parties also tended to have people with a higher probability of participants acquiring HIV.

Port soon realized that the people who had the most power behind these parties were the ones who supplied the drugs to everyone. It wasn't long before he started to deliver the drugs to people hosting these parties. The drug dealer would get to choose who was able to come to the party and also be able to have sex with whoever they wanted, usually just for giving them free drugs.

These parties were advertised on the gay hookup apps such as *Grindr*, and often there would be a time that you could show up and get in or out. Let's say the party was listed at 8 p.m. − 9 p.m., so you would only be allowed in during that time. Once 9 p.m. came, the doors were locked, and nobody was allowed in or out. People would take their drugs of choice, remove their clothing, and start the party.

This type of party was the perfect place for Port to find his victims. He preferred having sex with men who were unconscious and not responsive. He surfed the internet for pornography which showed this kind of fetish, got worked up, then went to a chemsex party as the drug supplier. He chose the victim he wanted, got them high, and had sex with that person. After a while, this wasn't enough to fulfill his fantasy. So he would lure his victim back to his apartment, where they would be alone. There, he could give them an overdose and go even further than he was able to go in the sex club.

Port either didn't know how much of the drugs he could give his victims, or he intentionally gave them too much. Either way, they ended up dead.

Also mentionable is that in 2019, Port's drug supplier Gerald Matovu was arrested and convicted of the murder of Eric Michels. He was sentenced to life imprisonment with the possibility of parole after 31 years served. It is believed that he was the drug dealer who supplied the GBH Port used in his murders of the four men.

2

DRAWINGS

Stephen Port Drawing #1

Stephen Port Drawing #2

PART II

THE MURDERS

3

ANTHONY WALGATE

Early on the morning of June 19, 2014, the police received a phone call about a dead body found in front of an apartment building on Cooke Street.

999 Dispatcher: *"Emergency ambulance, what's the address of the emergency?"*
Phone caller: *I think it's Cooke Street. There's a young boy. I think he's collapsed outside, and I don't know."*
Dispatcher: *"Outside of which number?"*
Caller: *"Um, 47 or 58."*
Dispatcher: *"Sorry?"*
Caller: *"47 or 58."*
Dispatcher: *"47 Cooke Street."*
Caller: *"Yeah."*
Dispatcher: *"Right, What area?"*
Caller: *"Barking. Looks like he's collapsed or had a seizure or something, or he's just drunk."*
Dispatcher: *"Okay, what's the telephone number you are calling from?"*
Caller: *"I'll go get my car."*
Dispatcher: *"Alright, don't worry about that. What's the telephone number you are calling from?"*

The caller puts the phone down and goes quiet.

Dispatcher: *"Hello!?"*

The 999 dispatcher calls the caller back.

Dispatcher: *"Hello, it's the ambulance*

service. We were cut off there. Could you confirm your location?"

Caller: *"Ahh, I've just driven away now."*

Dispatcher: *"Where was the fella outside of?"*

Caller: *"Uh, Cooke Street."*

Dispatcher: *"What number?"*

Caller: *"Um, I don't know, I didn't look."*

Dispatcher: *"You said 47 before?"*

Caller: *"Yeah, I did 47, yeah."*

Dispatcher: *"So you think they had a seizure? Is that correct?"*

Caller: *"Umm, uh yeah, yep."*

Dispatcher: *"So you were passing by in your car?"*

Caller: *"Yes."*

Dispatcher: *"Okay, and you've drove past now, so you're no longer there?"*

Caller: *"That's right."*

Dispatcher: *"How old did he look to you, sir?"*

Caller: *"Twenties."*

Dispatcher: *"Do you know if he was awake?"*

Caller: *"No."*

Dispatcher: *"Do you know if he was breathing?"*

Caller: *"No, I don't know."*

Dispatcher: *"Did you see anything happen at all?"*

Caller: *"No."*
Dispatcher: *"No, you just think he may have possibly had a seizure, and he was lying there on the floor?"*
Caller: *"Yes."*
Dispatcher: *"Okay, thanks for letting us know. We'll get someone there as soon as we can."*
Caller: *"Okay."*
Dispatcher: *"Thank you."*

The caller hangs up on the dispatcher again, so the 999 dispatcher calls him back.

Dispatcher: *"Hello, Sir. It's the ambulance service. Sorry to bother you again. It was definitely Cooke Street that the patient was on?"*
Caller: *"Yes. I passed him, and it was Cooke Street."*
Dispatcher: *"Okay, and were you just driving past and saw the patient lying there?"*
Caller: *"I was just driving out of my car park."*
Dispatcher: *"Is your car park there?"*
Caller: *"And I saw him lying on the floor."*
Dispatcher: *"Okay."*
Caller: *"I got out and had a look at him."*
Dispatcher: *"Yes."*
Caller: *"Called you and got back into my car."*
Dispatcher: *"Alright, no worries, no worries,*

just wanted to be sure. Thank you for your help,
sir, and sorry to bother you again."
Caller: *"Okay, no worries."*
Dispatcher: *"Bye-bye."*

Two officers arrived on Cooke Street at the location they were given by dispatch and saw a man lying asleep on the sidewalk. One officer immediately jumped out of their car to see if the man was still alive, while the other officer looked around the area to see if he could find anything suspicious. The man was dead, and they saw no signs of any struggle.

The body was that of a young man who looked to be in his early twenties. He was sitting on the sidewalk with his back propped up against the outside wall of an apartment building. His shirt was pulled up and wrapped around his chest, which exposed his stomach. His pant zipper was left wide open. His head was facing downwards, looking as though he had been asleep. He might have been dragged by his feet while lying face down. Beside him was a black duffle bag and a bottle containing some liquid, but police could not find a cell phone at the location.

The ambulance arrived and took the body to the hospital, where he was officially declared deceased. The medical examiner performed an autopsy where it was ruled death by overdose of the drug GBH. They had also found a bottle of GBH in his pants pocket.

In London, Barking had become known as a place where you would see the streets and parks frequented by male prostitutes and drug addicts. It was also an area you would stay away from after dark. There had been several overdoses in the area, so finding a young man dead from an overdose on the streets wasn't all that unusual. But one thing that stuck out for the police for this particular death was that the victim's underwear had been removed and put back on inside out. He also had 14 bruises on his body, so they decided to do a small investigation to see if there was anything unusual about this case. The first thing they would have to do was identify the victim.

For the first few days, police were unsuccessful in finding out anything about the dead man until Anthony Walgate's downstairs neighbor/friend came into the police station and reported him missing. She had tried calling his phone for two days and never got an answer. She went upstairs to his apartment several times to see him, but he hadn't been home for at least two days, not since he went to meet the man from Barking, whom he had met online.

When the police asked her why he was meeting this man he had met online, she explained that it was for paid sex. After that, the police seemed to lose interest in her missing friend. Likely because he was just a male escort who hadn't returned home.

Anthony Walgate, 23, was in his second year of design, fashion, and art at the University of Middlesex. Police discovered that he had been running ads on the *Sleepy Boys* app as a male escort to earn extra cash during his time in college. He often attended fashion shows with his two best girlfriends and his mother. Walgate's body was found the day before his mother, newly remarried, left for her honeymoon to Greece with her new husband.

Police decided to investigate the phone number from which they received the tip about the body on the sidewalk on Cooke Street. They found it belonged to the same Stephen Port who had booked the appointment with Walgate the prior evening. Two detectives went to Port's apartment at 62 Cooke Street to get a statement on the details of Port finding Walgate's body.

Port told them he had gotten off working the late shift around 4 a.m. When he arrived home, he saw the body lying on the sidewalk of his apartment building entrance. Port said he tried to wake the man by slapping him a few times but got no response. Port also claimed the man was still alive as he heard him gurgling and making groaning noises. So he sat the man up against the apartment building wall, called the ambulance, and went into his apartment and bed.

Walgate's mother and friends decided to do their own investigating. They signed into Anthony's profiles on several gay hookup apps and tried to find the man he was planning to meet. They knew this unknown man went by the name "Joe Dean" and learned quickly that that profile had been deleted. They went to the police with this information, hoping to find out who this Joe Dean was.

Later that week, detectives learned that Port had booked an appointment under the profile name of Joe Dean with Anthony Walgate for an evening of sex. After Port booked that appointment, he searched online for drug rape pornography. Port went to the Barking Rail Station at 10 p.m. to meet Walgate and bring him back to his flat.

About ten days later, on June 26, the police returned to Port's apartment, took him into custody, and brought him back to the police station for interrogation. While being questioned about the details of his discovering Walgate's body, Port continued to answer with the same story. He never changed his story until they asked him if he had ever used the profile name "Joe Dean." Detectives told Port that they also knew he had made an appointment for sex with Anthony

Walgate that same evening of June 17 and that he had reported finding his dead body in front of his apartment building. Port continued to deny that the man he had rented for sex was the same man he had found dead in front of his building. Later that evening, during the questioning, he asked the detectives if Walgate had had a fit in his apartment, and if it was an accident, would it still be his fault?

Eventually, Port started to change his story and admitted to having hired Walgate off an escort web app, and after Walgate got to his apartment, he began using drugs he had brought with him. Port said that the two engaged in sex twice during the night. Walgate got dressed to leave but fell asleep while wearing all his clothing, including his shoes. The next day when Port awoke, Walgate was still sleeping, so Port didn't wake him and left for his job. When he returned from work, he found Walgate was still asleep. Port could not wake him. Later that night, he heard Walgate gurgling and making strange noises, so he panicked, dragged his body outside to the front of his apartment building, where he left him lying on the sidewalk, and then called the ambulance.

Detectives decided to arrest Port and charge him with perverting justice during a crime investigation—or lying to police on a suspicious death case in simpler terms. The charge was a way of keeping Port in custody until they could figure out the details behind Walgate's death. After Port's arrest, the police returned to his apartment to complete a search and removed his computer for later examination. Unfortunately, the police neglected to search Port's computer during this investigation. It is uncertain why. We would never find out whether it was incompetence or lack of caring about the victim. But if they had properly searched his computer, they would have found incriminating evidence. They would have found several web searches for "Unconscious boy," "drug and raped," "Gay teen knocked out raped," and "guy raped and tortured young nude boy."

Time passed, and the police didn't discover any new evidence or lay any charges, which upset Walgate's family and friends. A few said they called detectives frequently and were brushed off. One of Walgate's friends, China Dunning, said when she asked police if they had searched Port's computer, they responded by telling her that it was a costly procedure and probably not worth it.

During Port's trial for lying to the police, he admitted that he had Walgate in his apartment for sex and that Walgate took the GHB willingly. "When I met Mr. Walgate for sex, the young man had wanted to have some stuff to make him horny and high." Port claimed, "I saw that he had a little brown bottle." He said it wasn't until after Port returned from a night shift at the bus stop diner that he found Walgate stiff and rigid in his bed, making a gurgling noise. Port then panicked, dragged the body out of his apartment building, and placed him against the outside wall. Port did not check to see if Anthony was still alive, he just got into his car and started to drive, and that's when he decided to call the 999 ambulance service.

In a police interview that day, the jury heard that Port asked a detective: "Can I say for the scenario - if it was an accident, and if he did have a fit in my place, is that still my fault?" "Initially," Mr. Rees said, "the defendant denied having met Mr. Walgate but later admitted spending time in his flat with him, where Mr. Port claimed Mr. Walgate willingly took GHB/GBL."

Port was found guilty and given eight months in jail as a sentence, but only served three months before being released with an electronic tag on his leg until June 2015. The police then closed the case.

Kate Whelan, Anthony Walgate's aunt, made an emotional appeal for people to take care when using dating websites and apps. "It was four years ago, and a predatory serial sex fiend murdered Anthony at the age of 23 while he was attending university and had an exciting future. Our lives will never be the same. We live daily with trauma, shock, anger, and pain. Please be careful if you are using dating apps. The internet is fabulous, but be aware there are predators. Although your kids are young adults and you feel sensible, please reinforce the stranger danger warnings."

4

GABRIEL KOVARI

G abriel Kovari, 22, originally from Slovakia, left his home because he felt the people there were too conservative and intolerant. He first went to Spain, where he lived with Thierry Amodio as his boyfriend. After he broke up with Amodio, Kovari headed for London, where he ended up sleeping in the spare bedroom of his friend John Pape in Southern London.

Within a couple of weeks in London, he found a job and decided that he wanted to get an apartment, even though his friend Pape told him that he could stay for as long as he wanted. Kovari wished to have his own place to meet men and have a private place to invite them back. About six weeks later, he told Pape that he had found a great place to live in the Barking area of London and was very excited to move there.

On August 23, 2014, he moved out of his friend John Pape's south London apartment. He texted Pape the Google Maps location of his new apartment, which was located on Cooke Street. A few days later, Pape texted Kovari to see how it was going in his new place. Pape received no answer from him. Two days later, Pape received a text message from Kovari saying things were good. That would be the last text sent from Kovari's phone.

On August 24, Ryan Edwards, who also lived at 62 Cooke Street and was a neighbor and acquaintance of Stephen Port, received a text message from Port inviting him over to meet his new "Slovakian Twink Flatmate." Edwards went to Port's place and partied with the two men all night.

The next afternoon, Edwards received a text

from Kovari, telling him that Port was not a very lovely person and that the two of them had had a big fight. Kovari didn't know what he would do as he couldn't live with Port anymore.

Later that same evening, Edwards texted Port and asked him how his new roommate Kovari was doing. Port said that Kovari had decided to move out and stay with some military guy he had met online on one of those gay dating apps.

———

Barking is a small town in East London, in the United Kingdom, with about 187,000 people. Primarily, it's a fishing and farming community. Barking came from the English slang for "Barking Mad," attributed to the alleged insane asylum attached to the Barking Abbey, which was part of St. Margaret's Church dating back to the 13th century.

On August 28th, the summer of 2014 was winding down, and East London resident Barbara Denham, 67, leashed her border collie named Max to take him for his daily walk. She always took the same route through the quiet and grassy property of St. Catherine's Church. It was the perfect place to walk as she could unleash her dog and not worry about car traffic or many people being around. This daily walk was something she had done for the 28 years she had lived in the area, and only this time would things be different.

When Barbara entered the Church grounds, things were as expected, only the sky was dark and grey, and the grass was damp from the rain that fell earlier that morning. She unleashed Max to let him run free and do his business as he always had done. She started to saunter towards the church, admired the architecture, and thought about how amazing it would have been to live in such an impressive building or castle. As she got towards the Abbey on the Church grounds, she noticed a young man sitting upright with his back against the stone wall. Barbara thought she would approach the man and say hi, but as she got up close enough to talk with him, she noticed that he didn't move. "I saw what I thought was a man sitting down on the grass, with his head slightly down and his back against the wall." Barbara claimed, "He was wearing dark glasses slanted over his face, and although I have seen a lot of homeless people sleeping in the area, I just knew something wasn't right."

Barbara clapped her hands and shouted out, "WooHoo." There was no response or movement from the young man. "He has a bluish pallor, and when I saw his eyes glassed over, I knew he was dead. There was no blood, and he looked very peaceful." Ms. Denham said she remained calm when she realized she had found a dead body. "I don't know whether it is watching horror programs or murder mysteries, but I was pretty calm. I took out my phone and called the emergency services, and they came pretty quickly."

This victim, too, had his shirt pulled up towards his chest, exposing his stomach, and was wearing sunglasses. His bags with all of his possessions were placed beside his body.

Two days later, her local paper announced that the young man she had found in the park, Gabriel Kovari, 21, had died of a drug overdose. East London was an area known for drug use and petty crime, so though it was a big shock to have found a dead body in the park, it wasn't a total surprise for there to have been a drug overdose in the area.

Police first contacted Kovari's friend, John Pape, by going to his apartment. They connected the two men as Pape allowed Kovari to use his address when he opened a bank account. The four officers told Pape that Kovari's body had been found in the park at the St. Margaret Church in Barking. Pape was able to give the police Kovari's parents information so they could contact them and let them know about their son's death.

Gabriel's mother, a pharmacist, described Gabriel as a gifted artist who wanted to make a difference. "He was full of love and cared for others and loved the company of his friends, and he was a very inquisitive and special child, gifted in arts."

After the police left Pape's apartment, he searched online for information about his friend's death. He learned online about another mysterious death in the same churchyard just a couple of months earlier in June. Pape couldn't stop thinking about the coincidence of the two young gay men both found dead in the same park about the same time, so he contacted Kovari's ex-boyfriend in Spain to chat with him about it. "I wanted Amodio to mention it to the police and make sure that they put the two deaths together."

Meanwhile, Anthony Walgate's mother was still following up with the detectives almost daily, wanting answers to her son's death. They often didn't respond or tell her they had no replies yet. When she, too, heard the news about another young man also found dead in the same park of an apparent overdose, she knew something was going on.

Around the same time, Stephen friended Gabriel Kovari's Spanish ex-boyfriend, Thierry Amodio, on Facebook, pretending to be an American student in London, Jon Luck. He did this to keep tabs on whether the police told him of any suspects and who they were.

Port told Amondo that he had spent a couple of nights with Kovari sometime around August 22 and wondered if the police might want to talk to him as his DNA might be found on Kovari's body. Port also claimed that Kovari was with Tony, an older Irish man who drove a Green Toyota. Amodio kept asking Port if he had more information about this Tony guy, and on September 19, Port told Amodio that he had found this Tony man who had been with Kovari. Tony texted Luck/Port, so Luck/Port asked him what had happened to Gabriel. Tony told him they were at a party somewhere in Barking and that Gabriel left with a young guy named Daniel, who was tall, thin, with light brown hair. That was the last time he saw Gabriel. Luck/Port told Tony that Gabriel was found dead, and Tony said he knew nothing about it and told Luck not to contact him again.

Shortly after this, the Coroner's Court reviewed Kovari's death. It was established that there were no signs of a struggle or any bruising or cuts to Kovari's body. Therefore, he wasn't in a fight or forced to take drugs. It was also revealed that there was no camera footage of the churchyard when Kovari went to the park and died. They also had no evidence from any of Kovari's clothing, as it was sent along with his body back to his home country so that his parents could bury him.

Kovari's landlord and friend, John Pape, was the only person to show up to the court as his parents didn't want to travel to London. He brought up three young gay males found in the exact location, all dead from apparent overdoses, and asked if the detectives had ever tried to investigate the possibility that all three deaths were connected. The inquest finished with an open verdict.

Two days later, Amodio texted Luck/Port back to tell him that the police had found another dead body of a man in the same park at the St. Margaret Church in Barking. The man's name was Daniel Whitworth—a young gay man who overdosed and had a suicide note on him.

5

DANIEL WHITWORTH

A bout three weeks after Barbara Denham found the body of Gabriel Kovari, she was walking her collie Max again in the same park. She noticed another young man sitting in the same place where she had found Gabriel. "This man was sitting the same way, with his head down as if he was sleeping." Right away, Barbara thought, "Please God, no, not another one. Please let him be a boy who is just drunk or something."

"I suppose I knew before I went over that he was dead. I just knew. " Barbara exclaimed. "But I touched his ankle where his skin was exposed and felt it was cold." She took her cell phone from her purse and called the police. "I'm the lady that found the first body. I have found another young boy."

"To have found two young men in the same position upset me. I was concerned about my reaction because I was trying to control myself. I did feel sorry for both, for the families. Someone else found a third body on the other side of the wall. I don't know how soon after I saw the second one." Barbara said with shakiness in her voice. "It was lucky I didn't find that one as well."

The second body she found was Daniel Whitworth, 21, from Gravesend in Kent, where he lived with his boyfriend, Ricky Waumsley, and worked as a chef, becoming very well known in the area for his cooking skills.

Both men were found dead in the same place in the same park, but Whitworth's body had a suicide note placed beside him. The suicide note suggested that he was responsible for the death of the first body found (Kovari) by overdosing on the party drug GHB during a sexual encounter.

Whitworth committed suicide as he could not deal with the guilt of what happened.

The note should have connected the two deaths for the police detectives, though, for some reason, it didn't. The police took the note at face value, and no further attempts were made to investigate his death.

Whitworth was sitting against the graveyard wall on top of a blue bedsheet, probably dragged like the previous two dead men found in the park. His shirt was also pulled up around his chest, exposing his stomach. Police could not find his cell phone on his body or anywhere in the park. They also found a little bottle containing some liquid, which was later tested and found to be GBH.

The police went to Whitworth's home to inform his boyfriend Waumsley that they had found Whitworth's body in the park. When the detectives asked Waumsley if the two were friends, Waumsley told them they were in a long-term committed relationship. Detectives then asked him if he knew that Whitworth was seeing other men. Police also suggested that Whitworth was using gay sex apps and GHB.

After the police left, Waumsley went online, looked through the gay dating apps, and found that Whitworth had profiles in several places. It came as a surprise because it was not in his character or behavior in any way. Both Waumsley and several of his coworkers and friends didn't believe the story that he had committed suicide after killing another young man with an overdose during sex.

After their investigation, the Barking Police would deem the death as non-suspicious and rule it suicide since they believed the note found on his body. Whitworth's stepmother claimed the police came to her and told her that her son had died of a drug overdose, despite no investigation and no explanation of the bruises found under both of his arms.

SUICIDE NOTE:

> *I am sorry to everyone, mainly my family, but I can't go on anymore. I took the life of my friend Gabriel Kline, we were having some fun at a mate's place, and I got carried away and gave him another shot of G. I didn't notice while we were having sex that he had stopped breathing. I tried everything to get him to live again, but it was too late. It was an accident, but I blamed myself for what happened, and I didn't tell my family I went out. I know I would go to prison if I went to the police, and I can't do that to my family, and at least this*

way, I can least be with Gabriel again. I hope he will forgive me.

BTW Please do not blame the guy I was with last night. We only had sex, and then I left. He knows nothing of what I have done. I have taken what G I have gone with sleeping pills, so it's what I deserve if it does kill me. I feel dizzy (misspelled on purpose) now as I took 10 minutes ago, so I hope you understand my writing. I dropped my phone on my way here, so it should be in the grass somewhere. Sorry to everyone. Love always, Daniel P.W."

I am Sorry to everyone, mainly my family but I cant go on anymore, I took the life of my friend Gabriel Kline, we was just having some fun at a mates place and I get carried away and gave him another shot of G I didnt notice while we was having sex that he had stopped breathing, I tried everything to get him to breath again but it was to late, it was an accident but I blame myself for what happened and I didnt tell my family I went on to, I know I would go to prison if I go to police and I cant do that to my family and at least this way I can at least be with Gabriel again, I hope he will forgive me.

BTW, please do not blame the guy I was with last night, we only had sex then I left, he knows nothing of what I have done. I have taken what g I had left with sleeping pills so if this kill me its what I deserve. feeling dizzy now as took 10 min ago so hoping you understand my writing.

I dropped my phone on way here so should be in the grass somewhere

Sorry to everyone

Love always

Daniel P W

Suicide Note

The police never questioned the suicide note and sent copies of a small part of the note to Whitworth's parents, asking them if they could verify that the handwriting belonged to their son. Even though both parents agreed that the handwriting looked like it belonged to their son, the written words were not the way their son talked or wrote. That was good enough for the Dagenham Police. They accepted it as verification that it was an actual suicide note written by

Whitworth and therefore never sought any further analysis of the suicide note. Later, when Whitworth's parents saw the whole suicide note, they knew their son hadn't written it. They immediately told the police this and asked whether they had investigated anybody mentioned in the note. According to them, the response from the police was, "It is what it is, and you just have to deal with it."

The parents brought another issue to the police: the note said, "not to blame the guy that he [Whitworth] was with last night." They wanted to know who this person was. The police told them that it would be impossible to investigate the note in such detail and that they needed to accept that it was what it was, an overdose by a prostitute. The police would never search for that guy mentioned in the note or even try to trace Whitworth's movements during his last night alive. If the police had researched this mystery man, the investigation would have easily led to Stephen Port.

Around this time, Stephen Port appeared in court for the death of Anthony Walgate. He was being tried for the charges of perverting justice during the police investigation into Walgate's death.

During the trial, the defense attorney told the court that Port had always been a law-abiding citizen who maintained employment regularly and was not a threat to re-offend. The judge in the case questioned why Port had just not called for help when the original overdose occurred. Port's lawyer said that it was Port's fear of his sexuality being discovered by the public. He feared for his job as a bus station cook and that being gay would surely get him fired.

Port ended up with only an eight-month sentence, and when the Walgate family found out, they were outraged. Walgate's mother already believed that Port had murdered her son by this time.

Shortly after Port's conviction, the Coroner held court for the Daniel Whitworth death case. During this hearing, the court heard that Whitworth's suicide note was assumed to be written by Daniel, even though the parents said differently. There was a discrepancy in the investigation with the bruising discovered under his armpits and on his chest. The detectives claimed that it raised no concern or suspicion, yet the Coroner stated that the injuries would have had to have happened before his death.

Another discrepancy in the investigation was when the police didn't test for DNA on the blue sheet on which Daniel Whitworth's body was found. The court asked about the DNA results from the blue sheet. There were none. Detectives hadn't even run basic tests on the sheet. This fact was pivotal in proving that, at the very least, detectives didn't thoroughly investigate. Especially since they already had Port's DNA. We know Port's DNA was later found on the blue bedsheet Whitworth's body was placed on at the church gravesite. Port's DNA was also found on Whitworth's body, clothes, and even the suicide note. Since Port had previously been convicted of a crime, his DNA was in police files.

Despite this, like the Walgate court hearing, there would be an open verdict. There were too many unanswered questions for the court to conclude.

Later, some communications between Port and Whitworth were also found. The two men had met on the *Fitlads* website in August that same year. On September 3rd, Port suggested that the two of them go for a drink before having dinner at Port's apartment so that Whitworth knew he wasn't some psycho. About two weeks later, on September 18th, Whitworth was seen leaving his job where he told his coworkers that he was meeting a friend in Barking. It was the last time he would be seen.

Even in February 2015, after Port pleaded guilty to the perverting the course of justice in

Anthony Walgate's death, the police still never connected the murders of the other two young men. Actually, the prosecutor said there was no suggestion that Port bore any responsibility for these young men's deaths.

After Port's conviction, some of Walgate's friends spoke to the police again. They said he knew he was responsible for their friend's death. But the police responded by telling them that only two people knew what happened that night, one of them dead, and the other wasn't talking—a rather flippant and uncaring response from the police.

6

JACK TAYLOR

P ort served his eight months and was released on parole. He had to wear an ankle bracelet. When he returned to his apartment in Barking, he had to face his friends and neighbors as he didn't tell any of them about his crime, trial, or conviction. Port said to them that he was sent away for selling drugs. He knew they wouldn't believe he would get eight months for simple possession. Port now had to find a new job since they fired him after his conviction.

Initially, the first three victims were deemed not to have died in suspicious circumstances. Despite the local police force's LGBT advisory group reporting that there was a serial killer at large, the police told the families of the victims and the public that the crimes were not linked.

The fourth victim, Jack Taylor, was a 25-year-old forklift operator from Hull. He was applying to be a police officer. On the surface, Taylor lived a straight lifestyle and had several girlfriends. Only he knew his secret of being gay. He usually used the *Grindr* app to meet men on the side to fulfill his urges so that nobody he worked with would know.

Jack was partying with friends at a local nightclub until about 10 p.m. on Friday, September 13th, and then he decided to go home. Once he was home, he started cruising the Gay meeting apps, and somewhere around 2 a.m., he met and started chatting with Stephen Port.

During their conversation, Stephen asked Jack, "Do you take T?" "T" is a street name for crystal meth. This question became relevant in future court cases. Jack answered no; he had never done it. "The two decided to meet at the Barking Rail Station at 3 a.m.

After they met, Stephen walked Jack back to his one-bedroom apartment, where Stephen was thought to have spiked Jack's drink with GHB. After Jack passed out, he injected him with poppers and raped him. Later, Jack's body was left at the St. Margaret's Church, leaning against the same fence where the two previous bodies were found, only this time, it was on the opposite side.

When the police arrived, they found Taylor leaning against the brick fence, the same as the previous two bodies. And his shirt had been pulled up and rested around his chest. Taylor had a syringe in one of his pockets, a little bottle filled with liquid, and a couple of pills in another. It looked as if he had been dragged to where he lay.

Again, after a brief inquiry, the police ruled that Jack had died of an overdose—a self-inflicted overdose. And there was no connection between Taylor's death and the other bodies found at the park earlier.

However, Jack's two sisters, Jenny and Donna Taylor knew that their brother never used drugs and thought his overdosing wasn't right. Even weirder was that Jack was supposed to have overdosed by injection. Yet, the needle found on him had never been used. The sisters did not understand why the police neither tested any evidence for DNA nor tried to find out what Jack was doing in that area of town. He didn't live there.

After not learning anything from the police, except that their brother's death was an overdose and it was not connected to any other body found in the park, the sisters decided to investigate what happened to their brother. First, they searched the internet to see if anything was mentioned about their brother's death. They were surprised to find out about three other young men found dead from an overdose in the same churchyard.

They started to go through the details of Taylor's last weekend alive. They wanted to find out everyone he was with and go to all the locations he had been to that weekend. They found out that the area where Taylor went was known for drugs and male prostitution. But they both knew that he was not a drug user. In fact, he often spoke out against others who used drugs. It didn't fit that he would walk into a churchyard, sit down, and shoot up.

Taylor's two sisters went to the police about two weeks later to find out if they had discovered any new information about the case. They were shocked to learn that not only did the Dagenham Police have nothing new, but they weren't even investigating his murder. The detectives told them they just had to accept that their brother had overdosed. Since they discovered a syringe in his pocket, some white powder in a baggie in his wallet, and several needle marks on both of his arms, to them, it was an overdose. The police told the sisters that they wouldn't help them with any investigation or information.

Frustrated, the sisters decided they would go to press with the knowledge that there had been other suspicious deaths in the same area. The media's attention created a lot of pressure on the police to do more.

About two weeks later, the police agreed to take the sisters to where they had found their dead brother's body. While the sisters were at the Barking Train Station, they discovered a CCTV camera looking over the area. They asked if the footage was available for them to view. When they all sat down to watch the footage, the sisters were shocked to see their brother walking from the train station with another man. They asked the detectives why nobody had told them about the film footage of their brother. Instead of answering them, the police took offense that they were even questioning the police investigation.

The sisters took the footage to the media. After they reported that it was Taylor's sisters who found the footage and not the police and that the police did not investigate the other man seen with their brother on the last night of his life, the detectives decided to reopen the mysterious death case.

About two weeks later, a sergeant from the Barking Police contacted the sisters to let them know that they had also found footage that showed their brother entering the churchyard grounds with another man. The sisters requested that the images of the man filmed with their brother that night be released to the press. But the police refused. Detectives told them they didn't feel that Jack's death was suspicious, so it wasn't possible to show someone's image on the news.

Again, after the two sisters went to press and more pressure mounted, the police released the pictures to the media of Jack Taylor walking with a tall blonde man at Barking Station on October 13th. They asked for the public's help in identifying who the man was. It was only two days for the police to find out that the man was Stephen Port. Surprisingly, it wasn't the public who identified Port but a police officer who already knew him.

Donna Taylor, Jack's mother, said the police should be held accountable for all the men's deaths. She accused the police of "class, gender, and sexual bias" and has suggested that lives may have been saved had they acted sooner.

After forensic psychologist Nadia Persaud examined each of the four bodies, the inquest returned an open verdict. A forthcoming ruling means that there is a need for more questions to be answered for them to conclude the reason for the deaths. Nadia said, "The most concerning are the findings by the pathologist of manual handling before the deaths. One of the bodies was wrapped in a bedsheet, sunglasses on another body's face and bottles of GHB were on or near all four of the bodies, and none were tested for fingerprints or DNA."

On the morning of October 15th, Stephen Port was arrested at his apartment for suspicion of administering poison to four men causing their deaths. DCI Tim Duffield interviewed Port from the Met's Homicide and Major Crimes Unit over the next four days.

PART III

JUDGMENT DAY

7

INTERROGATION

Barking Map with Port's Apartment &
Locations of the Bodies Found

During the interview, Port repeated his previous story about Anthony Walgate and finding him on the sidewalk outside his apartment.

Port claimed that he met Whitworth at a sex party at an East Londoner drug dealer he knew but said he knew nothing about the man or his death. He claimed to know nothing about the other two men. But as the interrogation continued over the four days, he changed his story and slowly admitted to his involvement with all four dead men found in the churchyard park.

The following are the actual transcripts of the interrogation of Stephen Port.

INTERROGATION OF STEPHEN PORT

Police Interviewer (PI) Tim Duffield: "So, did you have any involvement in the death of the male that we spoke about just a short while ago, Gabrielle Guevara or Gabrielle Kline?"
STEPHEN PORT (SP): "No, I did not, no."
PI: "Were you involved in administering any drugs or poison or noxious substances to him?"
SP: "No, I don't administer drugs to anyone or give drugs to anyone. Um, that's done at the party by someone of the name organized."
PI: "Who is that, sorry?"
SP: "Daniel. He organized it. Sometimes he is the dude that hands out the drugs to the guests."
PI: "Daniel?"
SP: "Yeah."

The detective moved a picture across the table face up towards Port.

PI: "Daniel, this is the man that you spoke of earlier?"
SP: "I don't know. I mean, it might be the same guy, I don't know, but he's the only Daniel I know."

There was a short pause as Port continued to look down at the detective's papers in front of him.

SP: "Like he does what I did, he'd pick up guys and bring them to the party."
PI: "Yes."
SP: "But he would stay longer and would administer drugs, hand out drugs, or whatever, but I would leave, and he would stay."
PI: "And did you go with Daniel to meet people?"
SP: "No, No, I knew he was doing the same as I was, but I would see him at the party, and I had a brief conversation about it, but I never actually engaged with him outside of that."
PI: "Outside of the party?"
SP: "That's right."
PI: "Which parties were these?"
SP: "All sorts, Frat parties."
PI: "Frat parties."

Another pause in the conversation occurred until Port covered his mouth and coughed a few times.

PI: "So when was the first time you met the person you are talking about, the man you know as Daniel?"

SP: "It was on the first few occasions I was there with Rafa Scott. Daniel was there. I don't even know if it's the same Daniel that we are even talking about. He is the only Daniel I can recall as such; he's the only one that rings a bell."

PI: "You think his name was Whitford?"

SP: "He was tall, almost as tall as me, brown hair."

PI: "It might help you if I showed you a picture. We call this CRT."

The investigator started directing Port's attention to the pictures he had placed on the table in front of him.

PI: "You see, this is Jack Taylor."

Port slid the picture of Jack Taylor towards himself and took a long quiet stare at it.

SP: "I don't pay full attention to the guy's faces when I have been to the parties, but I don't recognize his face."

PI: "So you don't recognize his face?"

SP: "No, I do not, no."

PI: "That's Jack Taylor, so you don't recognize Jack Taylor?"

SP: "No, I do not."

PI: "So, have you ever slept with this man?"

SP: "No."

PI: "Or had sexual intercourse with him?"

SP: "He doesn't look like the type I would go for myself."

PI: "He's not the sort of person you would go for?"

SP: "No, I don't want, he's more yoga-drinking boys, and he looks older. He doesn't look like some of the boys I've taken to parties, and he's not one of them."

PI: "So you don't recognize him as being one of them?"

SP: "No."

PI: "No? Okay."

The detective then picked up the photo of Jack Taylor and put it away amongst the other papers and photos on the table.

PI: "Again, Jack was found dead on September 14, 2015. Stephen, did you have any involvement in his death?"

SP: "I did not, no…no."

PI: "Did you kill Jack Taylor?"
SP: "I did not, no…. no."
PI: "Did you administer any drugs or noxious substances to him?"
SP: "No, no."
PI: "To cause him harm?"
SP: "No….no, I did not, no."
PI: "And you say you've never seen him before, is that right?"
SP: "That's right."
PI: "That's right."

The detective left the room for a short break. When he returned this time, he had several maps with him. He sat down and started placing the maps around the table.

PI: "What I've got right here is several maps. It's not easy to get it all on one piece of paper. Just so we're clear here, again, it shows your home address, and it shows you the church, St. Margaret's, and then behind it, you've got the Abbey and the primary school. The walls around the Abbey, have you ever had any reason to go into that area?"
SP: "No."
PI: "Have you ever been through into the Abbey?"
SP: "Ahh, no, I haven't, no. Those are touchy

areas. I once went to the church with my ex Danny on Christmas day, went to the church, but that's as far as I got."

PI: "You've not been into the grounds behind it, where you've got the old Abbey, the walls, or the grounds there?"

SP: "No, it looks spooky, so that I won't go there."

PI: "You've never been?"

SP: "No."

PI: "In all the eight years that you've lived across the road from that park?"

SP: "No, that's all private, so I wouldn't go there. It's a private area. It belongs to the church."

PI: "This is fairly open when you go past. Would you agree with that or not?"

SP: "At the field, yeah, the field is, but the church is behind the walls. I won't go past there."

PI: "Because three of the four people that have been found dead were found there. Slumped up against the wall near the Abbey."

SP: Softly mumbled, "Yeah."

PI: "What was that?"

SP: "I didn't know that."

PI: "You didn't know that? So that's news to you, is it?"

Stephen then remained quiet, placed his hands folded on his lap, and looked down at the church map on the table. What sounded like short sighs kept coming from him as he started to rock back and forth.

PI: "Did you put them there?"
SP: "No."
PI: "You see, Anthony (Walgate) was found outside your address with a large amount of GHB in his system. The other three men we've discussed were all found over by the wall area."

The detective then took his pen and circled the places where the bodies were found.

PI: "On the Abbey, you can see on this map again that they were slumped against the wall with a large amount of GHB in their body. Can your account for that at all?"
SP: "No, I don't."

The detective then flipped the map over and brought out another page. The detective now had a suicide note retrieved from the third victim Daniel Whitworth's hand.

PI: "Did you write this letter here?"

The detective then pushed the page over towards Stephen.

SP: "No, I did not."
PI: "This letter was found with Daniel (Whitworth)."
SP: "No."
PI: "Are you telling me the truth, Stephen?"
SP: "I am telling you the truth, yes."
PI: "Now all of these boys, young boys, all found dead, Stephen, in the early stages of their youth and their early twenties."
SP: "What do you want me to tell you?"
PI: "Close to your house. One of them had been in your house, either just before the time when he died and was found to have large quantities of drugs in his system. The other three were found just over the road in the churchyard, or just beside the churchyard in the area that we've discussed, propped up against the wall, a short distance from your house, all again with high levels of GBH in them. Enough to kill them is a highly unusual way to die for one person. This is four."
SP: "Right."
PI: "All found very close to where you live, all men, young me, the type of men you say that you find attractive, all now dead, Stephen."

Stephen remained very quiet, still with his hands in his lap and looking downwards, not facing the detective.

SP: "As far as Anthony I know, the other three, I don't know how they come to be."
PI: "Stephen, this is serious okay?"
SP: "Yes, I know."
PI: "You must tell us the absolute truth."
SP: "What I've said was true."

ANALYSIS OF INTERROGATION

Stephen Port showed many signs of anxiety in police interviews which helped officers convict him of the four murders and several rapes. Port scratched his nose while being questioned. His voice had a shallow volume, indicating that his words did not match the confidence levels behind them. Port's body language showed constant signs of anxiety when the volume of his voice dropped with every answer.

Dawn Archer, a professor of Linguistics, argues that there are indicators that Port was lying. *"Guilty speakers will use more negation, his volume drops, which suggests that a level of confidence doesn't match the words he's saying. In other words, he does not believe what he's saying."*

Experts also tell us that it's a sign of anxiety when your volume is meager during interviews. When we tell lies, we distance ourselves from our lies with our volume.

Port said "No" 40 times out of 47 questions

asked by the police. He kept closing his lips to ensure he didn't say too much. He also kept crossing his arms not to leak information. Port clenched his right fist and squeezed his hands. His body language showed us his tension and that he was feeling under pressure.

By the time the questions were more challenging for Port to answer, he was almost inaudible. For example, the interviewer asked Port if he was telling the truth about the boys, *"The type of men you say you find attractive, all dead now, Stephen."* Port replied in an almost inaudible low tone, *"Apart from Anthony, I know nothing about the other three or how they came to be."* Port squirmed his body around the chair and clenched his hands, telling us that he was hiding something. He then told the detective that everything he had told him up to this point was valid.

Stephen Port was charged with four counts of murder. Once the press reported on Port's arrest for the murders of the four young men found in the park, another eight men came forward and said that they too were drugged and raped by Port in his apartment. All of them had met him on a gay hookup app online. Many described Port spiking their drinks and injecting them with a small syringe usually meant for children when they were sick.

Eventually, Port was charged with eight more sexual offenses against the men who came forward to the police. He was convicted on seven of those charges but acquitted on one. In four of those cases, he was also convicted of rape.

8

TRIAL, CONVICTION, & APPEAL

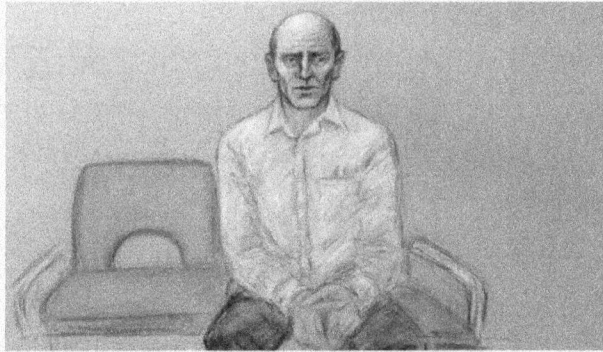

Hand Drawn sketch of Stephen Port
While on Trial

S tephen Port's trial began on October 9, 2015,
at the Central Criminal Court of England
and Wales, commonly known as the "Old Bailey."
Part of the prison stands on the road named after
the Old Bailey. It is on the site of the medieval

Newgate Gaol that was around since the sixteenth century. Old Bailey Street follows the line of the city of London's ancient wall, which was part of the bailey, or castle. The actual court building on this property was built in 1902. This crown court deals with major criminal cases within the Greater London area. The trials held in the Old Bailey are open to the public; however, they are subject to stringent security procedures.

The first day Stephen Port was brought into the courthouse, the grounds were full of screaming people, some crying and calling him names. Port just looked up at the Lady Justice statue on the top of the court building.

Placed around the walls of the entire hall is a series of references, some of them from the Bible. Port read parts of these phrases repeatedly while he was trying not to pay attention to any of the people yelling outside the courthouse and especially to keep from catching the eye of one of the victim's family members.

66 *The law of the wise is a fountain of life."*

The welfare of the people is supreme."

Right lives by the law, and law subsists by power."

Poise the cause in justice's equal scales."

Moses gave unto the people the laws of God."

London shall have all its ancient rights."

Most people were shocked at Port's appearance. He no longer had the hairpiece he had worn on his head for over ten years. His drug-induced party life had taken its toll on him, and he looked way beyond the 41 years he had lived on Earth. He would not once look at any of the victim's families or friends throughout the whole trial.

Prosecutor Jonathan Rees QC started by telling the Court that Stephen Port would meet men through websites and phone apps such as *Grindr*. He informed that the case would feature graphic evidence of a sexual nature and that they should approach it calmly, dispassionately, and analytically. The prosecution said, "This is a case about a man, the defendant, who in the pursuit of nothing more than his sexual gratification, variously drugged, sexually assaulted and in four instances killed the young gay men he had invited back to his flat."

Rees continued, "Port described himself as 70% gayer than straight with a preference for young, smaller boyish type men often referred to as "Twinks." His appetite for penetrating drugged young men was reflected in the drug-rape pornography he watched, and he occasionally filmed himself having sexual intercourse with the unconscious males. He had the propensity to render young gay men unconscious with drugs without their consent so he could have sex with them in that state. That was his inclination, his fetish, and what turned him on."

Rees then listed the drugs that Port had used on these young men as "Poppers or bottles of Amyl Nitrite, Viagra, M, also referred to as Meow Meow, T or Tina, the name for crystal Meth, and G, which was either GHB or GBL in its liquid form." Rees continued by saying that "GHB is of significance in this case. The postmortem examinations on the four young men who died revealed that each had died from a drug overdose featuring higher levels of GHB."

Rees finished by saying, "Each of the victims was found outside, very close to Port's apartment —three of them in the St. Margaret's churchyard." Rees said that the three victims found in the churchyard were propped up against the brick fence in the same position and with their shirts pulled up as if they had been dragged to their resting spots.

Rees then reminded the jury of Port's first arrest, "It was after the death of Anthony Walgate that Port was arrested and convicted for perverting the course of justice after he made false claims to the police. He had falsely denied ever having met Gabriel Kovari and Jack Taylor. Port also denied writing the wrong suicide note found in Daniel Whitworth's left hand."

Rees continued by stating, "The defendant allegedly met with Walgate, a fashion student and male escort, through the website *Sleepy Boys*, offering him £800 for an overnight. He met him at the Barking Train Station at 10 p.m. on June 17, 2014, using the name "Joe Dean." Rees said, "Port was a male escort. According to one of his former partners. Port described himself as having a big sexual appetite and particularly liked men in their late teens. Walgate had sent a friend a text giving this friend full details of who he was meeting just in case he got killed."

Rees stopped and looked at the jury members one by one slowly before continuing, "Around 30 hours later, at 4 a.m. on June 19, 2014, Port called the emergency services to report a young boy was collapsed or had had a seizure or was drunk on the street outside his flat. Port did not give his name and claimed he was just driving by and saw the man."

"Police and ambulance attended, and a doctor pronounced Walgate dead shortly before 8 a.m. although clearly, he had been dead for some hours. The body contained a bottle containing GHB, and the postmortem revealed high levels of GHB in Walgate's blood and urine within the range at which deaths from GHB intoxication have been reported," said Rees.

Rees continued his story but now looked like he didn't believe what he was about to say. "Port was discovered by police, who rung him back on his phone, asleep in his bed. Port then told the officers that he had found the man lying unconscious and had propped him up against the wall as he thought the boy had had a seizure, and then went into his flat and fell asleep."

The Court then heard about the eight living victims who allegedly were drugged and sexually assaulted by Port. The prosecution said, "It offends common sense to suggest that it was just an unfortunate coincidence that all of these men happened to either die or be sexually assaulted from an overdose featuring high levels of GHB, shortly after meeting with Stephen Port."

The first victim of Port that the police could find was only 19 years old, who met Port in February of 2012 through the app *Grindr* and was invited to his flat. The man claimed to have suddenly passed out and awoke to find Port having sex with him, to which he didn't consent. The victim later conveyed to a counselor that his drink must have been spiked and he had been date-raped by Port. The victim also told some of his friends about the attack.

Rees explained to the jury, "There are similarities in these circumstances with the case of another man who, three weeks earlier, had been seen with Port at Barking Station in a state of distress and unsteady on his feet, incoherent, and vomiting. Port had told the station ambulance and police he had found the 23-year-old under the influence outside his home. The prosecution explained that Port drugged him at his flat after the two men met through the *FitLads* website by giving him a clear liquid, which he thought was water, that caused him to fall unconscious.

Rees said, "He was deliberately drugged so the defendant could engage in sexual activity with him while he was unconscious." When the man woke up, he found himself naked and lying on the floor. Port then helped him get dressed and walked him to the Barking Station. "There is a common factor underlying the explanation of why each victim suffered an overdose, and that common factor is the defendant. The considerable efforts to cover up his connection with each deceased indicates that he, rather than the deceased themselves, was responsible for the fatal overdoses." Rees continued by saying that Port also tried to cover up his connections to each of his victims. "Each victim's mobile telephone was missing, and in each case, the defendant lied to the police about his knowledge of and involvement with the deceased."

Port pleaded not guilty to the four murders, the four counts of administering poison with the intent to endanger life or inflict grievous bodily harm, or the seven counts of rape.

When Port took the stand, he constantly mumbled his answers and often had to be asked to repeat what he said. Most of his replies were just one or two-word answers and often weren't relevant to the question he was asked. The prosecutor began to look like an angry schoolteacher trying to get one of their students to recite something from a book. "Speak up, please!" "What did you say?" or "Please state your answers more clearly." Throughout the cross-examination, he kept a blank unemotional look on his face. His eyes appeared dead.

Prosecutors asked Port about the videos they found on his phone and why the men appeared unconscious. He responded by saying that the police were showing you the last part of the videos and that there were several hours of him with the person he was having sex with within the video having regular sex.

A critical point during Port's questioning in Court was when he was asked why he lied about knowing or meeting the four dead men. He responded by saying he only lied because the truth sounded unbelievable, and he knew the police wouldn't accept it.

The Court heard that when detectives finally searched through Port's computer, they found evidence that Port pretended to be Jon Luck while he was chatting with Kovari's Spanish ex-boyfriend. It was divulged to the Court that Port did this to try and keep tabs on the investigation of Kovari's death. The police also checked through Port's cell phone and found 83 homemade movies of himself having sex with other men. More incriminating was the fact that several of those men were unconscious during the video.

In the case of Daniel Whitworth, a handwriting expert testified that the suicide note found on his body was definitely not written by Whitworth and was very similar to Port's handwriting. Even more damning was the Court hearing how the paper on which the note was written came from Port's apartment. The police also tested the blue sheet Whitworth's body was left on and found Port's DNA. It was proven to be from the bed in his apartment.

On the stand, Port eventually admitted to

writing Whitworth's suicide note but claimed that Whitworth actually dictated to him and he just wrote out what he said. Port also admitted to having met Jack Taylor in the same church park where he was found dead and that they had had a two-hour drug-induced sex session. He said Taylor was really into using drugs.

On November 23, 2016, after the seven-week trial, Stephen Port, 41, was convicted of the murders and rapes of Anthony Walgate, Gabriel Kovari, Daniel Whitworth, and Jack Taylor. He was also convicted of the rapes of three other unnamed men whom he had drugged and ten counts of drugging men without their knowledge or permission.

Port was sentenced to life imprisonment with a whole life order, meaning he will never be released on parole. During the sentencing, the judge commented, "I do not doubt that the seriousness of the offense is so exceptional that a whole life order is justified. I decline to set a minimum term, and the defendant will die in prison."

The police had problems keeping order in the halls surrounding the courtroom when Port was sentenced. The cheers and screams were loud, with several people shouting that they wanted Port to die.

After the trial was over, Malcolm McHaffie, Deputy Chief Prosecutor for CPS London, told the press, "Stephen Port committed many murders and rapes against young men. Port would control these men through the calculated use of the drug GHB, which he administered without them being aware. This was a complicated and challenging case but assisted by the large amount of evidence found on Port's many social media sites. The details of each of the deaths were strikingly similar as each of the victims was aged between 21 and 25 and had died within a short time of meeting Port. Port had engaged in sexual activities with all of them, and they had been killed of toxicity from drugs, and in three cases, a bottle of GHB was found in the circumstances with being planted."

Port's family still maintains that he is innocent. Port's mother has told the press that she knows her son is a kind boy and did not murder anyone.

Port was sent to HMP Belmarsh prison, a Category A prison that holds some of Britain's worst killers. He would meet Richard Huckle, Britain's worst pedophile, during his stay there.

The two of them struck a friendship and eventually a sexual relationship. When asked by the press how the two men could have had a sexual relationship in prison, the HMP Belmarsh replied that though both men resided in the max part of the prison, their cell doors were left open for the inmates to mix. The free time for the prisoners to mingle lasts about 90 minutes daily, and because they only have three guards to watch over them, things could happen. There was far too much for the guards to see everything that happens all the time. Both Port and Huckle have been moved but are probably still in contact by letters through the mail.

Port has expressed openly to several people that he hopes Hollywood makes a movie about him and that he gets someone like Kevin Bacon to play him in the film. There is currently a *BBC* TV series called *Four Lives* and actor Stephen Merchant plays Port. The series was originally named *The Barking Murders*, however, it was renamed to honor the victims. Port is unhappy with the choice as he believes that Merchant looks nothing like him. He is also apprehensive about the movie blackening his name and making him a target for attacks or even being killed by other prisoners.

Port's sister, Sharon, has told the *Sun* newspaper that the movie will make him look bad and that the movie makers couldn't know the truth. Therefore, it'll all be lies. "This will only make my brother look evil, but he's not evil."

9

APPEALS

On Thursday, August 30, 2018, Stephen Port, now 46, appealed against his convictions for the murders of four young men but did not appeal the several other convictions of sexual offenses against seven other living victims. A judge had to review Port's documentation to the court and decide whether to give the applicant permission to proceed.

After lodging his appeal, Port sought legal advice. He thought the charges were too high and untrue. Port figured that, if anything, he should have been convicted of manslaughter as these deaths were a series of self-inflicted drug overdoses. He also claimed that it was proven in court that each victim had other drugs in their system, including alcohol, before they even met Port.

Part of the claim said that Port should have been more mature and assertive with the men when they took the GHB, but most people who know Port claim that he is very young in the head but no murderer.

The families of the victim's spokeswoman immediately responded that it changed nothing and that Daniel Whitworth, 21, Anthony Walgate, 23, Gabriel Kovari, 22, and Jack Taylor, 25, were all drugged and raped by Port. Also, after killing the men, Port tried to cover up his crimes by disposing of their mobile phones, lying to the police, and planting the fake suicide note on the third victim's body.

On November 16, 2018, the judge dismissed Port's application to appeal at the first stage, ruling out the need for a panel of judges to hear his case. Jack Taylor's sisters, his fourth victim, said they were glad the appeal was dismissed because of the worry it caused them. It was quite a shock to them to learn that he had appealed the case in August.

INQUESTS INTO THE DEATHS OF STEPHEN PORT'S VICTIMS

In October of 2018, it was decided that a judge would be appointed to conduct the inquest into all four of the deaths related to Stephen Port's conviction in 2016. It followed a request by the current coroner, Dr. Shirley Radcliffe, to allow the inquest to be held in a different area or for her to step aside in favor of a judge. The results are expected to be in the hands of the victims' families sometime in 2019.

There has been genuine public interest in the outcomes of these inquests, especially since the original 2015 inquests into the deaths of both Gabriel Kovari and Daniel Whitworth were quashed. Those earlier open conclusions were reached when police had not connected the four men.

The victims' families were required to cover the legal costs of the inquests being conducted for their murdered family member. Jack Taylor's sister Donna told the *BBC* in September 2018, "We are trying to raise as much money as we can to have the best legal representation possible during the inquests because we think that, with what's happened, with the way we've been let down by the police, that we feel that we are going to need that." But she thinks it's unjust that the police are assured of public funding for their legal representation while the families are not. "It's ridiculous after everything we've already had to go through, especially from our point of view to fight for this from the very beginning, to then find yourself in a position of having to do this now. It's just ridiculous. The boys were murdered, there's a huge amount of police failings, and under these circumstances, it shouldn't be like this," Donna said.

Mandy Pearson, Daniel Whitworth's stepmother, agreed. "The police are dipping into public money. They can do it, no problem, and we've got to fight for what we need. A lot of this should be funded for us because, in the first place, the police didn't do their job. Otherwise, Stephen Port would have gone to prison, we would have felt justice had prevailed, and we would have left it at that."

Mandy also thinks much more significant changes are needed. "There are so many families in our position that can't afford the legal costs, so there should be something there for bereaved families. We're not just fighting for us; we're fighting for changes in this law, where we should be funded. We're looking for changes all along the line."

The families also applied for legal aid under the "Exceptional Case Funding Scheme," but it's uncertain if they qualify for the assistance. The government revised the legal assistance so that caseworkers consider when granting legal aid with the intention that funding would be more likely for those whose loved ones kill themselves or suffer an unnatural death while in the state's custody, such as in prison or a mental health unit.

The families raised over 10,000 GBP from donations from over 300 people on a successful crowdfunding campaign on social media.

In another twist to the case, newly disclosed documents from August 2018 revealed that Stephen Port was awarded 135,383 GBP of taxpayer's money to cover the appeal of his four murder convictions. It is deplorable considering the victims' families were left to their own devices to raise funds for their costs surrounding the trial and legal fees.

PART IV

LETTERS FROM PRISON

10

I'M INNOCENT! I AM BEING FRAMED BY THE MEDIA!

One of the more intriguing parts of this case is the information we can get from Stephen Port's letters from prison. He professes his innocence without hesitation throughout his letters, but so do most convicts in prison. He often claims that the victims had taken the drugs themselves throughout many samples I have placed here, and he hadn't administered them. He claims he might have sold the drugs or given the drugs to them but didn't inject any of the victims. So, at best, he should only be charged and convicted of selling or supplying illegal drugs.

Port also claims that the drugs found in the bodies of the dead men were only used to enhance their sexual performance. They all took the drugs willingly to have a "great sexual session." So, there was no rape.

> I am trying not to think about my trial yet as I am not looking forward to how many people and press are going to be there. I really don't like being the center of attention, and definitely not under these circumstances. I have said to my legal team not to waste time trying to get me bail which would not be allowed anyway, and to just focus on my case, and yes, of course, my plea will be not guilty. I haven't and would never harm anyone, of that I am certain."

> I know I never killed anyone with drugs, but I feel sad that guys have

died from taking drugs, and guys still are dying every week from drug-related problems or end up in prison-like me. I will make it my life goal to campaign against drugs and make people more aware of the horrific effects are from the ones they say are not addictive."

" My pleas and case management hearing will be the 7th. Of January, and if it goes to trial, that will be in April 2016, but I believe the charges will be dropped by then when the evidence proves that it's accidental death, not murder and that I did not administer GHB to anyone."

> *Of course, I cannot do this until I am found not guilty, which I am certain they will as I know I am innocent and God will be with me as he knows I could never kill anyone. I do have a good heart, and I have always tried to help others, and I treat everyone with respect."*

11

WHO SHOULD PLAY ME IN THE MOVIE?

I t's amusing that Port mentions how the media is talking about him and making up several stories about him, and most of them are not valid. Then later in the same letter, he talked about selling his report to the press or newspapers, but only for a lot of money. He also wonders who could play him best in a movie.

" Not sure who could play me in a film. I have been told I look like a younger version of Kevin Bacon. So, maybe him or Eddie Redmayne (*The Theory of Everything*) and maybe the guy who played Captain America? Lol. My friend here looks like Ben Whishaw (Q on the James Bond movie). I would like to say that he could play me, but he's got dark hair, and he's short, so probably not. Who would? You choose for you? Who is your favorite actor?"

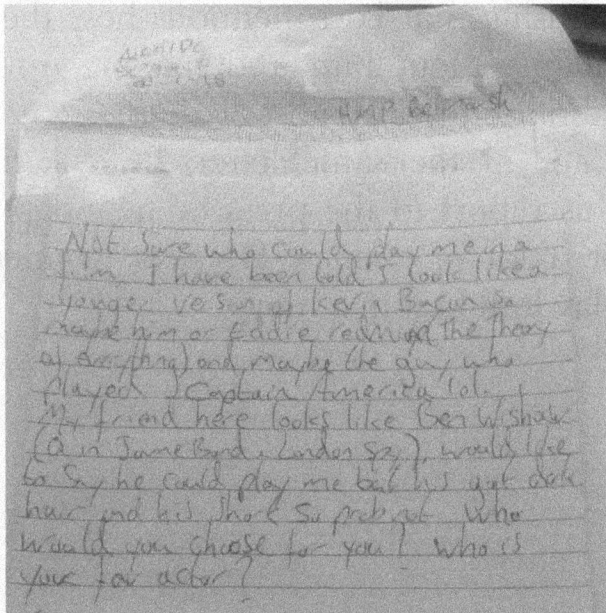

" When I do get released, there's going to be loads of media, but I won't talk to the press unless they offer me loads of money for my story. Lol."

" I'm not certain I could write more than two pages as there' not really that much of a k, but I would sell a story to the paper though I won't profit from it though, I would use every penny to make certain to make sure this never happens."

12

HOW TO BE A MALE ESCORT
AND NOT GET HURT!

Another part of Port's letters I find fascinating is when he tried to explain how to protect yourself from harm while being a male escort. One of his warnings was never to take a drink from a client since it could be drugged and make you pass out. You wouldn't want to be stuck alone in a client's apartment high on drugs as you could get raped or murdered.

The second point Port brought up was to make sure that you know the address you are going to and tell your friends the address where you are going, the name of the person you are supposed to meet, and the time you plan on arriving back home. They can report it to the police if you go missing afterward.

I guess it's pretty good advice to take when it's

coming from a man who has been convicted of raping and murdering four men he had bought for sexual encounters, all on the same nights he had met with them. They all showed a high drug content in their bloodstreams, having been raped and murdered by Port. So, if anybody would know what to watch out for, it would be Port.

" Have you slept with any of the famous guys you meet? I did have a couple of famous clients when *[I]* was escorting, but of course, I can't mention names, but they were generally MPS *[Minister of Parliament – Government leaders equivalent to Senators in America]*. Why do you want to be an escort? The money is good but be certain to check the client's details first. Most never give their real name. So, always take a PayPal deposit first. Normally so to make certain they are not wasting your time. Never do anything for less than 150 *[pounds]* and do not work alone. Give your partner the client's phone number, photo, address etc. Use your own lube and condoms and ask what they want to do first. Don't do anything extreme, like being tied up."

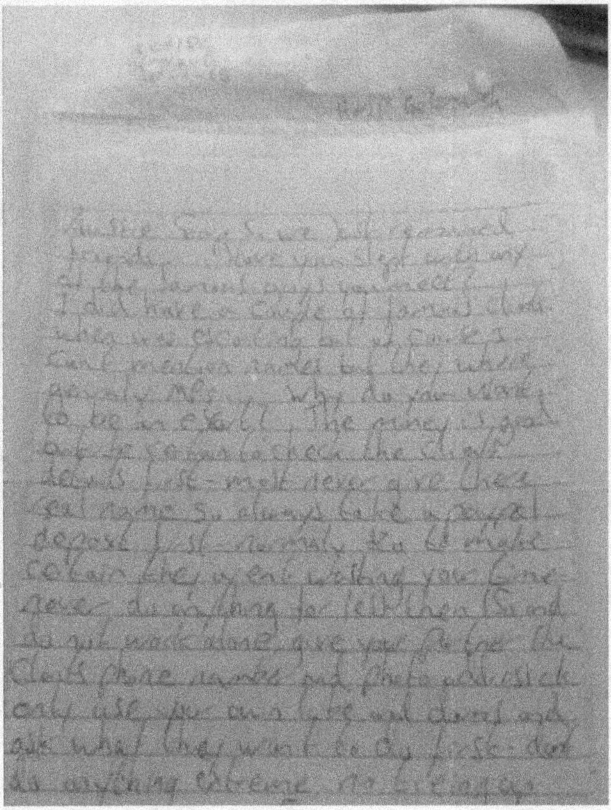

" Don't go to public places or any kind of restaurants as that's for a different type of escort which I would never do, always take your own drink and never accept any drink or food from clients. Take money first once he's happy with you and before you start anything. It's also advisable to go with your friend so the client can give the money to him and then he leaves. I know you're big enough to look after yourself, but never assume anything and always keep alert. Most escorts take their own drugs with them to make it more bearable but don't take them in front of the client and only use your stuff and only a small amount so that you're still in complete control. Never mention money and sex in the same email or text."

> Never mention money and sex in the same email or text. Always best to speak to the client on the phone first before arranging to meet. A couple of my older friends I first met when they were clients of mine, and one even became my flat mate when he was going through a divorce from his wife, which I believe I have mentioned before. Anyway, if you want to wait

until I am out of here, I will give you
some tips on how to make the client
happy quicker, but I won't mention
here as sure the person who has to
read this letter first doesn't want to
know those details. Lol."

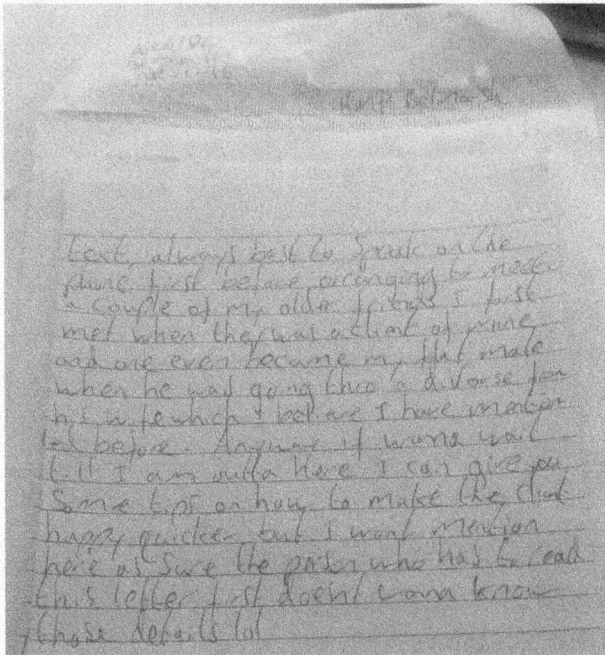

13

BEHIND EVERY SERIAL KILLER, THERE'S A BIG KID!

Another note was how frequently Port talked about his excitement in getting different toys and movies. His favorites were science fiction and fantasy stories such as *Star Wars* and the *Transformers*. He even mentioned once having an ex-boyfriend leave him because he collected toys. Port often asked if Cody would send him different toys and movies as he didn't have access to them in prison. You would think he would be focused on his trial and what everyone in the country was saying about him.

> Buy me the BB8 toy from *Star Wars* or the remote control flying millennium falcon and of course Yoda and Darth Vader fare. Yep, I know I am a big kid.

I once had a boyfriend who left me because I liked going into Toys R'us. He couldn't accept me still like collecting *Transformer* and *Star Wars* at my age. Lol. But we are still very close friends and had some mega amazing sessions together."

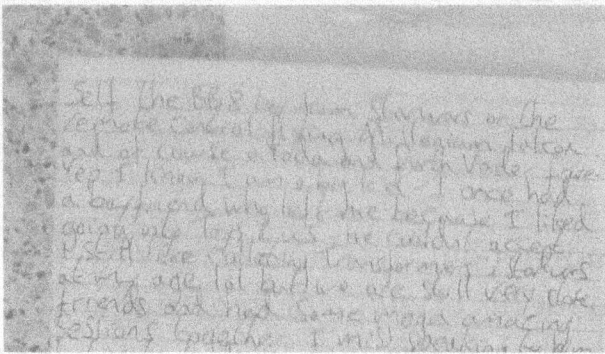

Do you have an American account? Instead of sending me a postal order, would you be able to order me some books/comics of Transformers Robots in disguise, please? Has to be sent direct from Amazon, though also a Pucca jigsaw with no more than 500 pieces, though. As I don't have a big enough table, I don't think they will let me have and *Transformers* or *Star Wars*, though, which is a shame."

Do you have an area can arrange instead of sending me a postal order would you be able to order me some books/comics of Transformers hopefully in if you could please? This to be sent direct to an American who also a puzzle no more than 500 pieces that don't have a big enough table don't think they will let me have any Star wars or Transformers figures that's which is a shame.

BB8 Star Wars

Pucca Jigsaw Puzzle

14

NURSE STEPHEN PORT?

Throughout Port's letters, he expressed the desire to dedicate the rest of his life to working for charities. Often he would say that his dream job would be to work for places like the Red Cross. Port also wanted to warn younger people about the evils and dangers of doing drugs. He would do this once he was found not guilty and released from prison.

I got the feeling that Port was saying these things as more of trying to prove his innocence because now that he had friends and partners who had died of drug overdoses, he felt it was his place to go out in the world to help others who found themselves in the same place he had been. He often attached these desires to help others with the expression "he would never want to hurt anyone" and that drugs were just a way of enhancing his sex life.

" My dream job would be to work for the Princess Trust, Red Cross, or any charity where I could make a difference and help others."

" When I do get released, there's going to be loads of media, but I won't talk to the press unless they offer me loads of money for my story. Lol. However, I would really like to use the media coverage to start a campaign to make people aware of the dangers of some drugs and educate people that drugs can kill."

"I never knew the dangers of GHB, and I don't believe many people really understand it could be lethal if mixed with alcohol or even prescription drugs and if you don't drink enough water when high. I just wanna get the message out there and also the dangers of doing drugs with strangers from online sites like *Grindr*."

15

NOVEMBER 5, 2015 LETTER

" Dear Cody,

Thank you so much for writing to me. It's the first letter I have had since my arrest, and I have not been allowed calls to my family, and I have no idea how they are coping. I have written them a couple of letters and asked if they could top up my canteen money as I only have seven-pound left after buying my essentials, coffee, biscuits, and some white chocolate.

The food here is alright but not enough. I was constantly hungry last week as after dinner at 4 p.m., there is nothing to eat until the following morning, and you only get a kid-sized breakfast pack. If possible, could you send me an A4 writing pad and a pen in a sealed packet? [according to Cody, that's for security] Please, as this pen is running out already, and I only got it on Friday.

Also, I know I'm being cheeky to ask, but it gets so boring just watching TV in my cell most of the day. I would be very grateful if you could send me a magazine. I like *Top Gear* films or *Star Wars* but anything would be nice. Hopefully, some magazine will have a picture that I can put up on my wall.

I like *Star Wars* and feel sad I won't get to the new film next month. I will pay you back when I get access to my account. I have a single cell as I am a VP prisoner. [VP prisoners are vulnerable prisoners – they would probably be attacked if they were put into the general population].

Everyone here has been alright with me, just the normal questions like did I do it or not etc., and I've been asked a few times to sign a picture of me in the paper, which is the only article I have read describing me as a serial killer which is so ridiculous, as a serial killer has intent to kill, and you can't intentionally kill someone with **GHB**.

How would it even be possible to give someone a high amount without them knowing [it], as it tastes vile? There's no way to disguise the taste, so the guy must know what he's taking and wants to be getting high on it. In the first place, it has a slow effect, so some guys take more before it's even kicked in and end up with a double hit.

However, some gays can take a large amount if they're used to it. My ex once drank a thirty-millilitre bottle full bottle of **GHB** when he was a wee bit high on M [methadone]. He was then rampant for a few hours but then took some more M, and he was back to normal, just with a sore throat as he didn't dilute it, so it burns his throat just a little bit. He was fine in the end. It's also quite addictive so wanting more is natural. If I wanted to kill someone, I would use an easier method like hitting over the head with a rolling pin.

I have been advised not to discuss

my case with anyone as I am being monitored, but it's common knowledge that I knew two of the guys. The first one I met online, and when he came around, he took his own G (GHB). I wasn't watching how much he was taking as he seemed to know what he was doing and measuring his own dosage, but I am certain he was on other pills. Maybe prescription drugs which acted bad with the GHB, which mixed any system.

They didn't mention that in the papers, anyway, I did call an ambulance when I saw he wasn't right, and I helped him outside to get some fresh air. He then sat down against the wall outside. I then saw the police arrive with an ambulance, so I panicked and went back inside.

A couple of hours later, the police came and questioned me and said he was dead.

I thought they were going to blame me and arrest me, so I lied and said I just saw him outside looking in and called an ambulance. But a few days later, they arrested me as they checked his phone and saw that he had arranged to meet me.

So, I got charged with perverting the course of justice, and I was sentenced to two months as a cut D prisoner in Brixton Prison and two months on psych.

The other boy I met at a sex party I got invited to from Grinder. I can't remember too much about it due to the number of free drugs on offer out of the party. I did overdo it a bit and remembered feeling sick. He and another guy asked where I lived and helped me home

I just fell onto my bed and passed out. I woke up after hearing a loud bang and a glass smash. I could also hear voices and shouting, but I couldn't move. I couldn't even turn my head. It was as if my body wasn't there, so I closed my eyes and slept until I woke up the following afternoon.

The flat was empty, just a broken glass, a spilt drink on the coffee table. I cleaned up and thought no more of it. Please excuse my bad handwriting. I don't have my reading glasses. I have told the nurse, and she said that she would make an appointment with the optician, but it could take three to four weeks and then it will be another couple of weeks to wait for the glasses to be made.

Why was you in prison? How long did you get? I was a head chef for a catering company but got dismissed when I was convicted [earlier for perverting the course of justice] back in March of 2015. I have been to Manchester a few times. I worked in Leeds for a short while a few years back and used to take day trips to Manchester with my boyfriend, who lived in York. [Cody Lachey had told Stephen Port in his letter that he lived in Manchester and used to be in prison] My trial is not until April next year, so I have a long wait here. I do hope that you will write to me again, and I will answer more of your questions when certain you receive this letter.

Many thanks.

Stephen Port"

A026104
Stephen Port
H4-1-16
H.M.P. Belmarsh   5-11-2015
Western Way

When writing to Members of Parliament please give your previous name and address in order to avoid delays in your case being taken up by the M.P.

In replying to this letter, please write on the envelope:

Number A026104   Name Stephen Port

Wing H4-1-16   05-11-2015

H.M. PRISON BELMARSH
WESTERN WAY
THAMESMEAD
LONDON
SE28 0EB

Dear Cody

Thank you so much for writing to me, its first letter I have had since my arrest and have not been aloud calls to family & S. I have no idea how they are copeing, I have written them a couple of letters and asked if they could help top up my canteen money as only have £7.00 left after buying essentials and coffee, biscuits and some white choc, the food here is alright but not enough, was constantly hungry last week as after dinner at 4pm there is nothing to eat till the morning with a kids size breakfast pack. If possible could you send me an A4 writing pad and a pen (sealed in packet) please as this pen running out already and only got it Friday. also I know being cheeky to ask but it gets so boreing just watching TV in

①

A026192
Stephen Port
H4-1-16
HMP Belmarsh   5 11

cell most of the day I would be very dred
ful if you could send a Magazine, I like
topgear, Film or Starwars but anything
would be nice and hopefully some mag will
have a picture I can put up on wall, I like
starwars and feel sad I wont get to see
the new film next month. I will pay you
back when I get access to my account.
I have a single cell as am a VP prisoner
everyone here has been alright with me.
Just the normal questions if I did it or not
etc, and was asked a few times to sign a
picture of me in papper which is the only
artical I have read disgribing me as a
serial killer which is so ridiculose as
a serial killer has intent to kill and you
cant intentionly kill someone with GHB,
How would it even be possible to give
someone a high amount without them
knowing as it tastes vile there no way to
disguise that taste so the guy must know
what his taking and wants to be getting
high on it in first place, it has a slow
effect so some guys take more before
its even kicked in and end up with a
double hit, However, some guys can
take a large amount if used to it, my
ex once drank a 30ml full bottle when

5.11.2015

he was a wee bit high on M, he was then campent for a few hours but then took some more M and he was back to normal, just with a sore throat as he didnt dilute it so burnt his throat a bit but he was fine, its also quite addictive, so wanting more is natural. If I wanted to kill I would use an easier method like hitting over head with rolling pin or something. I have been advised not to discuss my case with anyone as I am being monitored but its common knowledge I knew two of the guys, the first one I met online and when he came round he took his own G, I wasnt watching how much he was taking as he seemed to know what he was doing and measuring his own dossage but I am certain he was on other pills maybe presqiption drugs which acted badly with the G when mixed in his system, they didnt mention that in pappers. Anyway, I did cull an ambulance when saw he wasnt right and I helped him outside to get some air and he sat down up against wall outside, I then saw police arrive with ambulance so I paniked and went back inside, a couple hours later the police came to question me and said

Stephen Port
H4-1-16
HMP Belmarsh   5-11-20..

he was dead, I thought they was going
blame me and arrest me so I lied and
said I just saw him outside looking
ill and called an ambulance, but a
few days later they arrested me as they
checked his phone and saw he had arranged
to meet me so I got charged with prevent-
ing the course of Jastice and I did 2
months as a Cat D in Brixton and 2
months on bail. The other boy I met
at a sex party I got invited too from
Grindr, I cant remember too much
about it due to the amount of free drugs
on offer at the party, I did over do it a
bit, I remember feeling sick and he and
some other guy asked where I lived and
helped me home, I just fell onto my bed
and passed out. I woke up after hearing
a loud bang and a glass smash I also
could hear voices and shouting but I could
not move, couldnt even turn my head it
was as if my body wasnt there So I closed
my eyes and slept till woke up following
afternoon, the flat was empty Just a
broken glass and spilt drink on coffee table,
I cleared up and thought no more of it.
Please excuss my bad writing as I dont
have my reading glasses, have told the nurse

H4-1-16
HMP. Belmarsh   5-11-20..

and she said she would make appoint
ment with optician but it will take
3-4 weeks and then will be another
couple of weeks to wait for the glasses
to be made. Why was you in prison
and how long did you get??
I was a Head chef for a contract catering Company but got dismissed when
got convicted back in March. I have
been to Manchester a few times, I worked
in Leeds for a short while a few years
back and used to take day trips to Manchester with my Bf who lived in York.
My trial is not till April next year
so I have a long wait here - I do hope
you will write to me again and I will
answer more of your questions when
certain you receive this letter.
                    Mary thanks
         (5)   Stephen Port

16

DECEMBER 12, 2015 LETTER

Dear Cody,

Just received your letter dated the 19th of November. This week has been slightly better as I just started working in the ink shop, just filling up cartridges for printers, but time goes fast. So, the day goes a bit quicker, and the guys speak to me now, and they don't seem to be bothered about why I am here.

They just take me at face value. One guy I've been working with said he thinks I'm a nice, polite guy and said you don't seem like a murderer, and I told him I'm not and that I would sooner kill myself than take another's life.

Anyway, I only get two pounds, sixty a day Monday to Thursday, but at least it helps me buy essentials, but no luxuries though as just a pack of coffee is three-pound, ninety-nine and Jaffa cakes are pound. They're gone in one go as I love them, LOL. I finally have an optician appointment for Monday.

So, I should have my glasses soon, and my writing will become more readable, I hope. So, what have you been doing this week? I have lots of memories from my life. While being in here, I remembered a lot of things I haven't thought about in ages.

My childhood was quite normal. My dad was strict but never abused me. My mum is quiet but speaks her mind when she wants to. I always had what I wanted within reason. At school, I wasn't really bullied, but I used to get called stretch because I was tall and skinny. But at 16, I started going to the gym after reading some books on bodybuilding. After a few months, my arms and shoulders started to get a bit bigger, so I didn't look like a bean pole anymore. I became better at sports, and no one would bully me. [This is another contradiction as he just said he wasn't bullied, but when he worked out and became more muscular, nobody would bully him anymore?] I was quite shy, but I had plenty of friends as I was more of a jock because I was good at basketball.

My ex-boyfriend was disowned when he came out as gay at 14, put into care by his foster parents, and sexually abused and ran away until he was put into the care of his granddad's, who was 76. He did his best, but with him having autism and ADHD, he was very difficult with his moods. He could become very aggressive.

However, at 18, he met me online and at first, he would just stay a week at a time. His grandfather used to drive him down until I taught him to drive, and he got his own car. After two months, he moved in with me for the first year we had a normal relationship with normal sex. I know you are probably thinking that I am the older guy, but I never had supply him with drink and didn't know about drugs back then.

He was always horny and very loving, and we did everything together. He had his moods at times, and I had to call his grandfather to come down and help me as he would run out shouting and screaming in the street a few times. The neighbors would call the police, but it wasn't from anything I did, it could be from one of his friends online, or I got a text from a friend that would upset him. He would get jealous very quickly, as he wanted my full attention. Nobody else could have me. He didn't like change, and everything would have to be as he wanted.

During the second year, he met a friend online that was his age. It wasn't anything sexual between them, so I didn't worry. But he gave me methadone and said try it with Steven, your boyfriend. So, we did it to give a try. It was amazing, but after a while, he would want me to try other stuff, so his friend game him GHB. He was sick at first, but he kept wanting more. Then after a while, he started getting into the habit of taking GHB and being very submissive. He said do what you want to me. I trust you. He wanted me to have control over him, and he wanted me to tie him to the bed.

Also, I can only guess, as he was abused when he was young, that now it became a part of him. But instead of being forced to do it, he wanted it to be completely submissive. Sorry, I am rambling again. I know you want to know more about me and not my ex-boyfriends, but he was such a big part of my life for four years, that was back in 2013.

When we split up, we didn't remain friends, but he didn't get on that well with my new boyfriend. They would clash and argue, and they would both fight for my attention, so he went back to live with his grandfather, and the new boyfriend moved in with me."

[On Cody's previous letter, he told Port that he had been drugged sexually abused.]

Did you report this guy who

drugged you? I could never do that because what's the point of sex if you're both not enjoying it? I do prefer one on one sex rather than group sex, I liked his full attention, and I want to give him mine. It's so much better with kissing and cuddling, also which you don't do in a group orgy, it's just about getting in and coming etc. I prefer the real love.

I am being charged with administering a drug with intent to cause harm, which is murder times four. I was just charged with perverting the cause of justice as when my friend had a bad effect, I took him outside and left him there. When the police arrived, and I said that I didn't know him, as I was scared. They then accused me of taking drugs with him. Now they accused me of giving him the drugs to intentionally kill him, which is so ridiculous. He was my friend, and I would never do that, and I certainly didn't do that to my other friends.

It's most likely these guys had too much G at a party, and these guys took him to a park to avoid being done for drugs etc. or even maybe the guys enjoyed sex outside. I have done it in the past, and it's quite exciting in the fresh air.

Anyway, I am not allowed to discuss my case as these letters could be used as evidence. But I have nothing to hide. I have told the police everything I've just mentioned to you. My role models used to be Van Damme, Arnold Schwarzenegger and Chuck Norris and Sly Stallone. I took up martial arts and became a senior grade in Taekwondo-Do. I won five silvers in the British Nationals and a Bronze at the English Championships.

But as you've seen from my pics, I've never really gained big muscles, just slim and toned because I had a really good six-pack. I got a job as an underwear model for Jordan Conrad [British Fashion designer] Debenhams Range [a high-end department store], and I used to have long blonde hair, so I looked like a surfer. I did swimwear too.

I'm just looking back at your letter and trying to answer as many of your questions as I can.

I like *Doctor Who*, and I wish I had a Tardis, LOL. [A fictional time machine or spacecraft in the Dr. Who series] I like the stories and adventures, *Matt Smith* was my favorite, but after watching a few episodes with the new guy, I think he's amazing? He fits the part as he looks older. It makes more sense as he's supposed to be 2000 years old.

I did like David Tenant, though. I do like *Family Guy* and *Futurama*, but the main cartoons I like are *Transformers* and *Marvel Avengers*.

I have been to Manchester's gay village. I was in a club there on New Year's Eve/New Year's Day back in 2007. I think I was with a boyfriend who lived in York. I was overseeing an opening of a restaurant in Leeds. I was helping train the staff and managers. I was living in a Travel Lodge [hotel] paid for by my company. I used to take the boyfriend out for dinner and charge it to the company, and they never did know they were paying for two, LOL.

I will get my canteen ordered tomorrow morning, more Jaffa cakes yummy. Thanks again for sending the 25 pounds. I won't say no if you want to send me more HeHeHe. I really do appreciate your loyalty and friendship, and I wished you was my boyfriend. Can't wait to meet you when I get out of here.

Have a great weekend,
Best regards.
Stephen Port
kiss kiss kiss."

17

DECEMBER 15, 2015 LETTER

Dear Cody,

Thank you so much for the 25 pounds. I can order some shoes and some Christmas sweets. I only just received your letter dated 8th. [December] I don't know why it's taken nine days to get to me, but yes, they must be busy coming up to be Christmas. I finally have reading glasses so I can see to write better now and it's so nice wearing my own clothes.

If I were free now, I would go to the cinema to see the new *Star Wars* film and then go to Pizza Hut for a large ham and pineapple pizza. How was your birthday? What did you do? My favorite meals here is the cheese and macaroni, steak, and kidney pie. I like the chicken Tikka Baguette also. I don't like any of their mince dishes. The lasagna or mince beef pies are awful. It's a shame as lasagna was my favorite meal on the outside. I can make an awesome lasagna. I wish I was the chef here. I would definitely make some changes. I would improve the menu with better tasting food and do it within their budget or less as I can see they must waste a lot.

I am well and healthy, lost some weight though, I was 84 kilograms and now 80 kilograms. I try to keep fit. I do my abs at night before bed and use the gym Friday and Saturday, but now [that] I am working, I can't go outside for exercise. I used to run around the yard. Now I only get air on Friday and Saturday when I go to the gym. I miss that. So, it's just Sunday I get outside, which makes sleeping more difficult as the fresh air and exercise would help make me tired.

I am enjoying the work. It's good to be doing something. I chat to the other guys here. I have made a good friend here, we work together, and we sit in my cell and chat when we get some time, he was feeling really depressed as he wasn't getting on with his cellmates and not many others would speak to him. He said he didn't speak to me at first because he read in the papers that I hated gay guys and killed homosexuals, lol.

I told him no, I am gay myself, and my friend died of a drug overdose after a sex session and that I am being accused of giving him the drugs which led to his death, but I certainly didn't kill anyone. Anyway, he told me he was thinking about ending it all, but now we are friends, he's a lot happier. He's been here a year already and still on remand until April. Same as me. There's also a couple of other older guys we have started getting on well with and planning a card game at Christmas with some Quality Street [chocolate candies] for the winner.

My mum and dad are a lot better now as the police and media are leaving them alone now. They sent me 10 pounds, and dad has bought me some more new clothes, which I hope I will get once the prison checks them over. Still not been allowed a visit yet, though, which is quite depressing as I was hoping to see my sister before Christmas.

I am not sure about writing a book. Not certain I could write more than two pages as there's not really that much to fill a book, but I would sell my story to a paper. I would not profit from it, though. I would use every penny to make certain this never happens to anyone again. So, no other families have to lose a loved one to drugs or being imprisoned for administering GHB, just more awareness is needed.

I know it's impossible to stop people trying drugs, but if they are educated in the correct use of the, I believe lives can be saved. Of course, I can't do this until I am found not guilty, which I am certain they will, as I know I could never kill anyone. I do have a good heart, and I have always tried to help others, and I treat everyone with respect.

What have you got planned for

Christmas? I look forward to spending next Christmas with you in Manchester, what will we do? There's no Christmas cards on the canteen list so I can't send you one, but I will write another letter, and I will try to answer your other questions. They still won't let me have the boots you sent. My sister sent me the *Star Wars Annual* and the *Minions* book direct from Amazon. That really cheered me up!

Chat Soon

Stephen XXX."

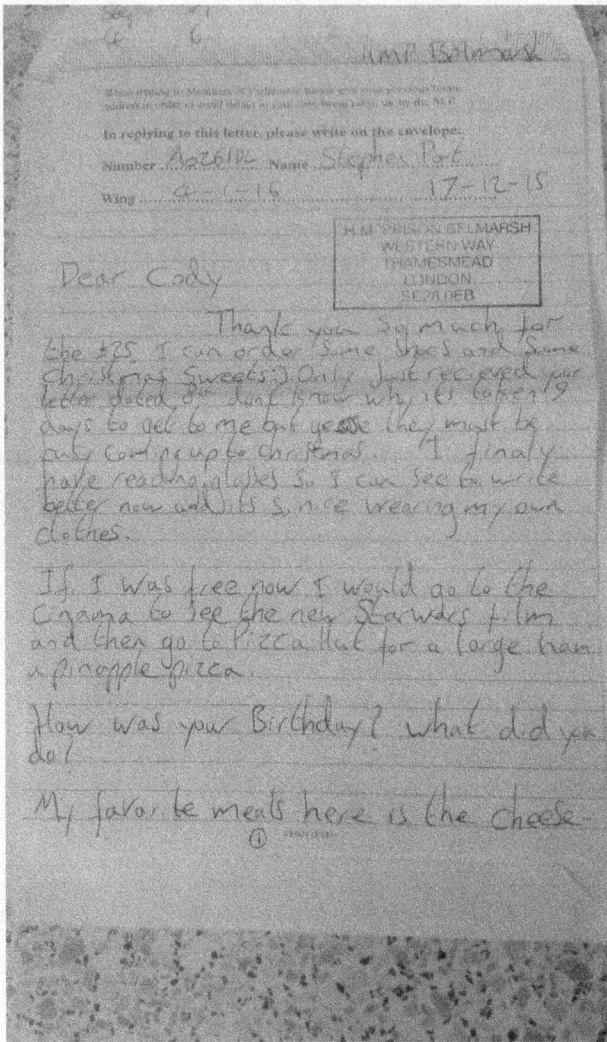

Sep 6
4 6

HMP Belmarsh

[When writing to Members of Parliament please give your previous home address in order to avoid delays in your mail being taken on to the M.P.]

In replying to this letter, please write on the envelope:

Number A2261PC Name Stephen Port
Wing 4 - C - 15   17-12-15

H.M PRISON BELMARSH
WESTERN WAY
THAMESMEAD
LONDON
SE28 0EB

Dear Cody

Thank you so much for the £25 I can order some shoes and some Christmas sweets. Only just received your letter dated 6th dont know why its taken 9 days to get to me but yesse they must be busy cooped up to christmas. I finally have reading glasses so I can see to write better now and its so nice wearing my own clothes.

If I was free now I would go to the Cinama to see the new Star wars film and then go to Piccallilli for a large ham & pineapple pizza.

How was your Birthday? what did you do?

My favorite meals here is the cheese
①

Macaroni, steak kidney pie + likes the
chicken (chilli bolognaise also. I don't like
any of there mince dishes the lasagne or
mince beef pies are awful, its a shame as
lasagne was my fav meal on the outside
I can make an all from lasagne. I wish I
was the chef here I would def make some
changes I would improve the menu with
better tasting food and do it with a close
budget or less as can see they must waste a
lot

I am well and healthy, lost some weight
tho, I was def heavier was 80kg, I try to
keep fit I do my abs at night before bed
and use the gym Fri + Sat, but now I
am working I can't get outside for
exercise, I used to run around the yard but
now I only get air on a Fri + Sat when
I go gym I miss that, its just Sunday
I get outside which makes sleeping more
difficult as the fresh air + exercise would
help make me tired, I am enjoying the
work tho its good to be doing something + to
chat to the other guys here, I have made
a good friend here we work together and
we sit in my cell and chat when get spare
time, he was feeling really depressed he
①

as he wasn't getting on with his cell mates
and not many others would speak to him, he
said he didn't speak to me at first cuss he
read in the papers that I hated gay guys
and killed homosexuals lol, told him no I am
gay myself and my friend died of a drug
overdose after a sex session and that I am being
accused of giving him the drugs which lead
to his death and I certainly didn't kill anyone,
Anyway, he told me he was thinking about
ending it all but now we are friends, he's a
lot happier, he's been here a year already
and will on remand until April same as me
there also a couple of other older guys we have
started getting on well with and planning a
card game at Christmas with some Quality
Street for the winner.

My Mam & Dad are a lot better now, and
the police & media are leaving them alone
now, they sent me £10 and Dad has bought
up some more new clothes which I hope I
will get once the prison checks them over
Still not been allowed a visit yet tho which
is quite depressing as I was hoping to see
my Sister before Christmas.

I am not Sure about writing a book or

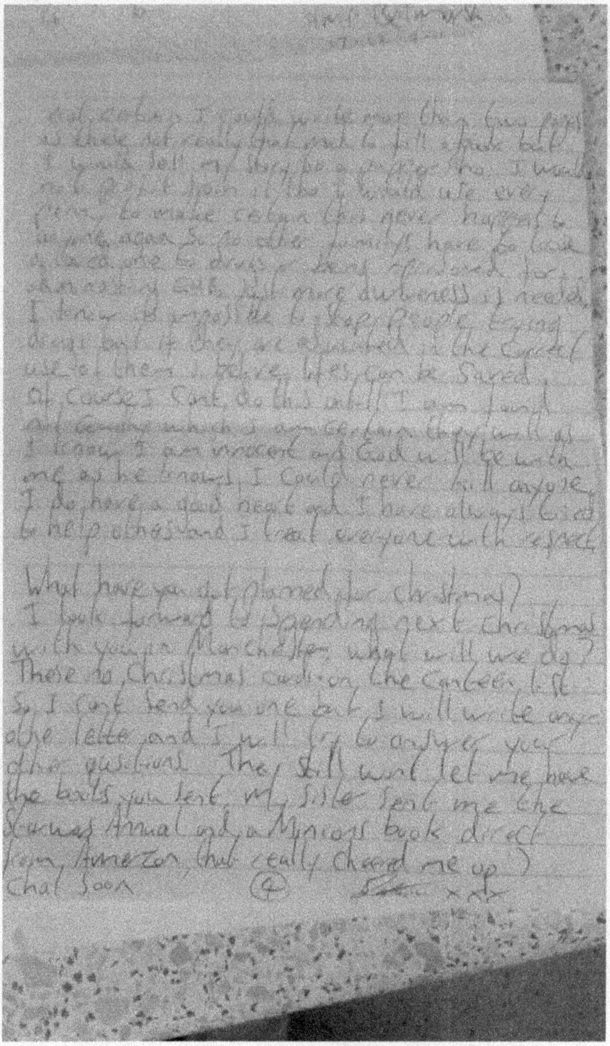

[illegible] I could write more than [illegible]
as there [illegible] really that much to tell [illegible]
I would tell my story for a purpose tho. I would
not [illegible] upon it tho I would use every
penny to make certain this never happens to
anyone again so no other familys have to lose
a loved one to drugs or being murdered for
something which just more awareness is needed.
I know its impossible to stop people taking
drugs but if they are educated in the correct
use of them I believe lifes can be saved.
Of course I cant do this untill I am found
not guilty which I am certain they will as
I know I am innocent and God will be with
me as he knows I could never kill anyone.
I do have a good heart and I have always tried
to help others and I treat everyone with respect.

What have you got planned for christmas?
I look forward to spending next christmas
with you in Manchester, what will we do?
There no Christmas cards on the canteen list
so I cant send you one but I will write anyo
other letter and I will try to answer your
other questions. They still wont let me have
the books you sent. My sister sent me the
[illegible] Annual and a Minions book direct
from Amazon, that really cheered me up :)
Chat soon (4) [illegible] x

18

DECEMBER 19, 2015 LETTER

" Dear Cody,

Thanks again for the 25 pounds. I have just one my canteen order for Thursday. I ordered some mince pies and a Christmas cake, Maltesers, Cadbury eclairs and yep, my favorite Jaffa cakes. So, I will have a good munch while watching *Dr. Who* on Christmas Day, and *Mrs. Brown Boys* should be fun. On Boxing Day, I will be watching *Shaun, the Sheep*, and after that, *Dickenson* and *Top Gear*. What will you be watching?

How was your birthday? Get any nice pressies? Any plans for Christmas? If you could have any present for Christmas, what would it be? Do you collect anything? If I was out now, I would buy myself the BB8 from *Star Wars* or the remote control flying Millennium Falcon and of course, a Yoda and Darth Vader figure. Yep I know I am a big kid.

I once had a boyfriend who left me because I liked going into Toys R'us. He couldn't accept that I still liked collecting Transformers and Star Wars at my age, Lol, but we are still very close friends and had some mega amazing sessions together. I miss speaking to him but not an allowed to as he was questioned by police as a witness, but he did write a really good witness statement and said I have always treated him well, and he always consented when we had a drug sex session together with the occasional threesome. He really enjoyed watching porn where a sub boy (over 18) was being used by older guys while he was high and enjoying ourselves.

This time last year, we were planning a Christmas session with a good friend of mine. We became boyfriends on New Year's Day. Going to be difficult this New years as I remember what an awesome time we had last year from Christmas Day New Year's Day. It was amazing, wish I could go back in time to then.

Anyway, I just have to look forward to next Christmas, but I will definitely be more idle and just stick to alcohol and avoid other stimulants. What's your best memory of past Christmas' and New Year's? When I was younger, living with the parents, I remember unwrapping my presents on Christmas morning. I used to get Star Wars and transformer toys etc., and console games. I know you said your childhood wasn't good, so when did you first have a good Christmas?

I am trying not to think about my trial yet as I am so not looking forward to how many people and press are going to be there. I really don't like being the center of attention, and definitely not under these circumstances. I have said to my legal team not to waste time trying to get me bail which would not be allowed anyway, and to just focus on my case, and yes, of course, my plea will be not guilty. I haven't and never would harm anyone, of that I am certain.

The lads here are fine, I have had no trouble from anyone, and I get on well with most of them. Just a couple I avoid. There's one guy who just comes into my cell and cuddles me from behind and rubs me so much. He did the same to my friend. We had to ask him to leave us alone. He is harmless and obviously gay. He's a lot bigger than me and shouts if annoyed, so we treat him carefully. He really should be in healthcare under supervision.

I am not on a Cat A-wing. There's a mixture on this VP wing and even a couple of Cat D who are being released shortly. My friend doesn't know what Cat he is but said he wasn't given one yet. Have a fantastic Christmas and New Year's. I look forward to hearing from you in 2016. All the best wishes.

Stephen Port xxx"

Dear Cody

Thanks again for the £25.
I have just done my canteen order for Thurs
I ordered Some mince pies and a Christmas
cake, maltesers cadbury eclairs and (yep my
fav Jaffa cakes.) So I will have a good
mooch while watching Dr who on Christmas
Day and Mrs Brown's Boys should be funny.
On Boxing day I will be watching Shaun the
sheep and after that Dickensian and Top
Gear. What will you be watching?

How was your Birthday? Get any nice
pressies?

Any plans for Christmas? If you could
have any present for christmas what
would it be? Do you collect anything?

If I was out now I would buy my

Anyway I still have to look forward to next half term and I will def be more fun the next if it be alcohol and good I near I mean!! What's your best memory of past christmas's and New Years?

When I was younger I being with the family, I remember unwrapping my Presents on Christmas morning such as get Scolextrics Transformer toys etc and so sle Aimes, I know you said your childhood wasn't good. So when did you last have a good christmas?

I am trying not to think about my trial yet as I am not looking forward to how many people and press are doing to be there I really don't like being the centre of attention and def not with those 6 glum stares. I have said to my legal team not to waste time trying to get me bail which would not be aloud anyway and to just focus on my case only 95% of course my plea will be Not Guilty, I never stand never would harm anyone. of that I am certian.

The lads here are fine, I have had no—

③

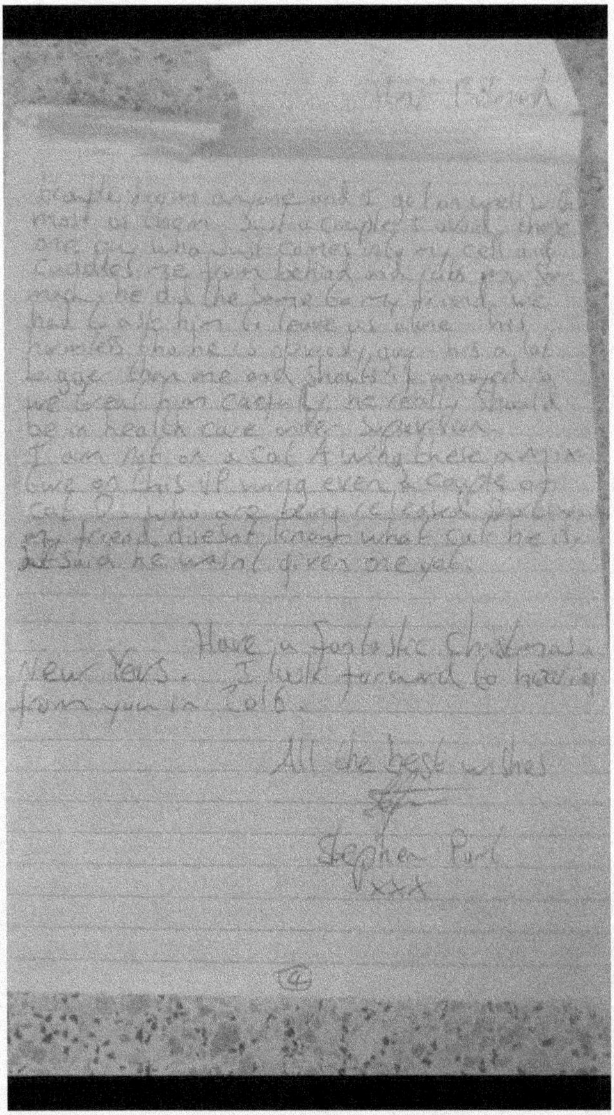

19

JANUARY 4, 2016 LETTERS

JANUARY 4, 2016 LETTER #1

66 Dear Cody,
    Thank you so much for the Darth Vader card. I love it. I got the Christmas canteen list today with Christmas specials on like Quality Street [chocolate candies] 3. 99, but my favorite Dan Cake Xmas Log 1.79 and Galaxy bar 1.39. So, if you want to send me an Xmas present postal order, I can order some as I got to do a two-week canteen order next Friday, but please only send if your certain you can afford it as I felt bad asking as

you're not working and I am sure you have enough bills of your own.

I am a Cat A but not on a Cat A-wing, there is all Cats on this VP wing, including Cat D. I am on remand with charges of administrating a drug with intent and working as an escort, but it is not true, as you have to keep alert as a client could drug you, have sex and not pay, that's why I never worked alone or accepted drinks and only used my own condoms and lube etc.

I think I am the only celebrity on this wing as there is no one I recognize from TV. One guy is doing the coke with the guy who he kept his daughter as a slave, which has been on the news lately. The guys here are all really nice and more talk to me, but there are a couple I stay clear of. They have been in fights, and when a couple of them kicked off when we were socializing, they locked us all back in our cells for the rest of the day. Everyone got punished, and it was just over a TV remote.

My solicitor, QC, and Barrister are coming to see me in the morning as the CPS papers have been served. I will make a longer letter to follow with more about me and the sex pictures etc. It's 11 p.m. now. Off to bed.

    Regards
    Stephen Port x."

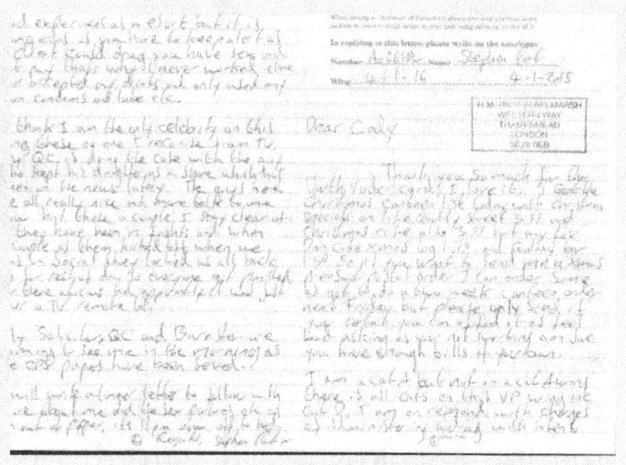

JANUARY 4, 2016 LETTER #2

  Dear Cody,

    Really nice to get your letter tonight. It's 10:30 p.m. now. I was just watching *Deutschland 83*. Have you been watching it? The main guy is really cute. When it first started last

Sunday, an agent drugged his coffee and knocked him out for a few hours. I don't think they should show things like that on TV as it could have given the wrong side to people as he woke up wearing new clothes, and he didn't even complain and ask why they did that.

Anyway, Happy New Year to you. I had a good Christmas, but New year was a bit depressing as I was alone when it struck midnight. I kept thinking about the year before when it struck midnight. I was spooning my boyfriend on the bed while fireworks were going off outside. It was so romantic and loving. He said it was his best high ever. It was for me too.

I am doing all right. It is nice having a close friend here. We cuddle often but nothing else as we never get any privacy together with other friends and officers walking in and out of my cell, but I am not that bothered by it as he is more like my little brother. I enjoy his company, and it's just nice to have that body contact when I hold him close. He's shy like me and tells me everything about himself and his case, not as major as mine, just some indecent images on his laptop etc.

But he is facing 91 charges, and his trial is also in April. I don't share his preferences, but I am not judging him as he's a decent guy, and he doesn't believe I did what I am accused of. Two new prisoners moved into his cell, so I didn't get a chance to put an app in to share with him. He asked me to ask you if you could please send him some airmail stickers, they are free from the post office as he wants to write to his friends abroad.

Would you be comfortable to write to him directly if I give you his details, or you prefer not to? I understand if you feel it could be awkward. He wanted to see my *Grindr* profile pictures. Do you have any from the papers? Could you send them to me, please? They might not let me have them, but you can try if possible.

Just would like to show him pics of me with blonde hair. Talking about hair, I don't think they would let me have my piece sent in, which is just against my human rights, but uncertain what the law is regarding that. Maybe you could check online and find out what the law is, but guessing as it's not medical, it won't be seen as relevant. If you do campaign for better treatment of prisoners, you could mention about being in a three-person cell. My bro barely gets any space or privacy and spends lock-up time just lying on his top bunk watching TV and reading papers.

Also, there's only three working showers between 75 prisoners on this wing. I never get a chance to get a shower. There's not enough social time to wait for one to be free, so at night I just wash down in the sink with shower gel and sponge. It's easier for me as in a single cell. I keep looking back at your letter to find which question to answer next.

My dream job would be to work for the Princess Trust, Red Cross, or any charity where I could make a difference and help others. The church area is a known guy cruising area and a place for those who enjoy outside jiggy jiggy, but I personally prefer it with a boyfriend inside unless on a private beach in the Grand Canary Islands, lol.

I don't gotta that area at night. It's spooky, but there's lots of homeless guys and druggies who sleep around there. When I get outta here, the first thing I am going to do is go to the pub for a pint of Guinness, then take my family and friends out for dinner to thank them for all their support and you so when I come to Manchester.

I only just sent my canteen sheet up this morning. I ordered Hariboloo, cookies 69, Jaffe's, coffee 3.99, peanut butter, lemonade. I only have a few quid left as spent most of it over Christmas as sharing all my sweets and cakes with friends. I would be grateful if you could send a postal order as I would like to buy a duvet cover and pillow to help me sleep better. My plea hearing is vis video link on the 15th.

The strange gut who cuddles me and my friend is still here. My friend is bit scared of him as he cuddles too tightly. I can take it as I am quite solid, but he's really skinny, so when this guy comes in, I sit in the middle of the bed, so he can't get behind him. He's as big as both of us put together, lol. He doesn't say much. He sits there just looking at us. Sometimes he will comment on whatever I'm talking about with friend/bro. Luckily he doesn't stay long, which is a relief.

What are your New Year's resolutions? Have you met any new guys recently? Off to bed now. It's 12:30 a.m. Please write again soon, look forward to hearing from you.

Best wishes,
Stephen XXX."

Cody Lachey
10/01/2016

Stephen Port
A6261DL
4-1-16
HMP Belmarsh

Dear Cody

Really nice to get your letter tonight. It's 6:30pm now, I was just watching Deutschland 83 have you been watching it? The main guy is really cute, when it first started last Sunday an agent drugged his coffee and knocked him out for a few hours, I don't think they should show things like that on TV as it could give the wrong idea to people, as he woke up wearing new clothes and he didn't even complain and ask why they did that. Anyway, Happy New Year to you - I had a good Christmas but new year was a-bit depressing as I was alone when it struck midnight, I kept thinking about the year before when it struck midnight I was spooning my boyfriend on the bed while fireworks where going off outside it was so romantic and loving, he said it was his best high ever, it was for me too. I am doing alright, it is nice having a close friend here, we cuddle often but nothing else as never get any privacy together with other friends and officers walking in and out of my cell but tbh am not that bothered as his more like my little brother. I enjoy his company and its just nice to have that body contact when hold him close, his shy like me but his always chatty with me and tells me everything about himself and his case, not as major as mine just some indecent images or

his laptop etc but his facing 91 charges
his trials also in April. I don't share
his preferances but am not judging him
as his a decent guy and he doesn't believe I did what I am accused of. Two
new prisoners moved into his cell so I didn't
get a chance to put in appin to share with
him. He asked me to ask you if you could
please send him some air mail stickers,
they are free from the Post office as he
wants to write to his friends abroad -
Would you be comfortable to write to him
directly if I give you his details or you
prefer not too? I understand if you
feel it could be akward. He wanted
to see my Grindr profile pictures, do
you have any from the pappers? Could
you send them to me please? They
might not let me have them but you can

③

by, if possible. Just would like to show him pics of me with blond hair. Talking about hair, I don't think they will let me have my piece sent in which is pis against my Human rights but uncertain what the law is regarding that, maybe you could check online and find out what the law is but guessing is its not medical it won't be seen as relivent. If you do campainge for better treatment of prisoners you could mention about being in a 3 man cell, my bro barely gets any space or privacy and spends lock up time just laying on his top bunk watching TV and reading pappers also these only 3 working showers between 75 prissoners on this wing. I never get a chance to get a shower these not enough social time to wait for one to be free So at night I Just wash down in the

Sink with shaver gel and sponge, its easier for me as in a single cell.

I keep looking back at your letter to find which question to answer next. My dream job would be to work for the Prince's Trust, Red Cross or any charity where I could make a difference and help others.

The church area is a known gay cruising area and a place for those who enjoy outside jiggy jiggy but I personally prefer it with a boyfriend inside, or unless on a private beach in Grand Canary islands lol. I don't go to that area at night its spooky, but these lots of homeless guys and druggies who sleep around there.

When I get outta here the first thing I am going to do is go to the pub for a

pint of guiness,then take my family and
friends out to dinner to thank them for
all there support and you also when I
come to Manchester.
I only just sent my canteen sheet up
this morning, I ordered, Haribo 1.00,
Cookies 59, coffee 3.99, peanut butter, lemonade. I only have a
few quid left as spent most of it
over christmas as shared all my sweets
and cakes with friends, I would be
gratful if you could send a postal order
as I would like to buy a duvet, cover
and pillow to help me sleep better.
My plea hearing is via a vid link on
the 15th.
The strange guy who cuddles me and
my friend is still here, my friend is
bit scared of him as he cuddles to-

⑥

Eightly... I can take it as I am quite solid but his really skinny so when this guy comes in I sit in the middle of bed so he can't get behind him his as big as both of us put together lol, he doesn't say much, he sits there just looking at us. Sometimes he will comment on whatever we are talking about with friend/bro luckily he don't stay long which is a relief...

What are your new years resolutions? Have you met any new guys recently?

Off to bed now its 12 30 am. Please write again soon, look forward to hearing from you...

Best wishes
Stepha xxx
:)

20

FEBRUARY 2, 2016 LETTER

Dear Cody,

I hope you are well. I have not heard from you in a while. I do hope you haven't given up on me, or I hope I haven't said anything to upset you. I miss hearing from you. I still have had no visits yet as my sister is still waiting for the forms. Not even be able to phone anyone either. It's all taking so long, I am sure you have heard that the trial won't be until October now as they don't even have enough evidence yet to go to trial in April, so my plea will be in April instead.

What have you been doing? Are you working now? After my ten-week trial, I look forward to starting afresh, my mortgage has been frozen, so at least I won't be in arrears when I go home after the trial. However, I will probably sell it and move to Manchester and maybe stay with you if you still would like me to but will depend what restrictions they put on me. [The Court]

I can't wait to see my friends and hopefully get back with my ex-boyfriend or find a new boyfriend. But for certain, I never ever want to touch another drug as long as I live. I just want a normal loving relationship like I used to have before. I didn't realize how much harm drugs really did to my brain, it's been over three months now since have had any stimulants, and for the first time in over a year, my mind looks clear, and my brain seems to be healing but still so much I can't remember, lots of blanks.

I wish I could go back in time to September 2013, which was the first time I ever tried real drugs when a friend Jake gave my ex-Danny a bunch of meth to try with me. Now I wish I didn't give into him. I just did not want him to do it alone or with some strange guy as I thought by doing it together, it would be safer. It was a lot of fun at. First, I admitted to that, but after six months, the effects were more minor, so we started taking more and adding E to make it stronger. It got to a point when I only saw him when he wanted to come around for a session. He would drive me back to Kent on the Monday or Tuesday, depending if we had anything left.

If I had known the damage, it would do to my brain. I wouldn't have ever been tempted to try it. I hope when I leave here, I can get the message out to stop anyone being tempted into drugs. I now know how it destroys lives, even though I was never addicted to it. It just became routine to do it with the boyfriends. I only ever did it when they wanted to, though, with their consent, he was autistic, not stupid, not like down syndrome. He was more than capable of telling me exactly what he wanted, and he loved sex and being high otherwise, he would not have kept coming back to me again and again.

Anyway, sorry, just a rant there as police using the "that he had some sort of emotional problems and saying I took advantage of him," which is so untrue. I loved and cared for him like any other boyfriend. Do you still take drugs, and do you go to orgies or saunas? What are your thoughts on drugs?

I know I never killed anyone with drugs, but I feel sad that guys have died from drugs and guys are still dying every week from drug-related problems or end up in prison-like me. I will make it my life goal to campaign against drugs and make people more aware of the harmful effects, even from the ones they say are not addictive.

I am doing all right here at the moment, although I only seem to be working in the mornings now. At lunchtime, I get locked back up and left for the rest of the day. I only get exercise and a socialize on Friday and weekends when I go to the gym with my friend, and we play backgammon and table tennis, which is good fun but wish we could have more time together. Look forward to hearing from you.

Best wishes,

Stephen Port XXX"

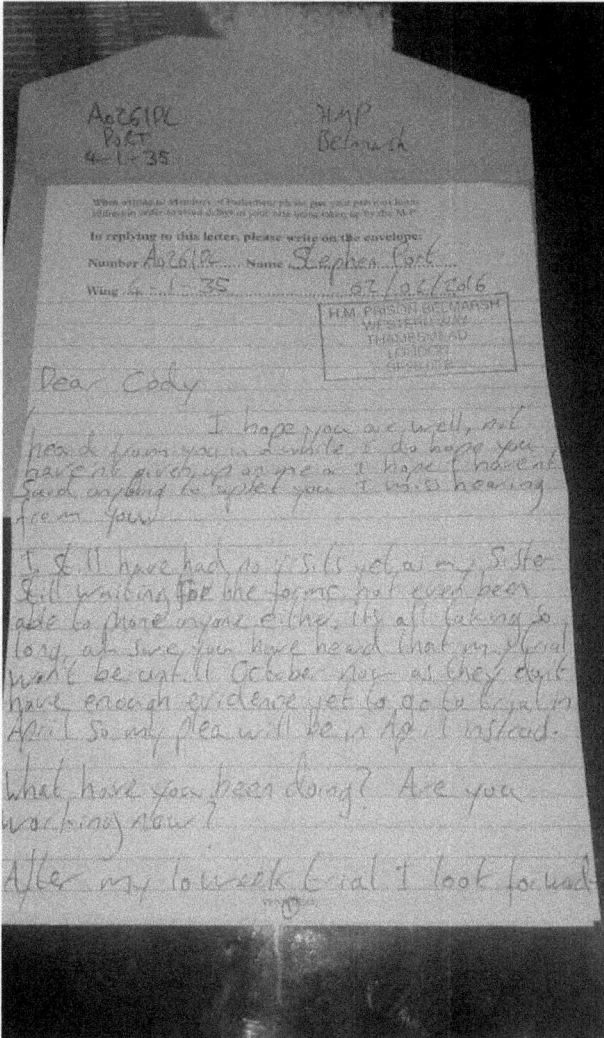

to starting afresh, my morgage has
been frozen so at least I won't be in
arears when I go home after the trial but
I prob will sell it and move to Manchester
and maybe stay with you if you still would
like me too but will depend what restrictions they put on me. I cant wait to
see my friends and hopfully get back
with my ex bf or find a new boyfriend
out for certain I never ever want to
touch another drug as long as I live, I
just want a normal loving relationship
like I used to have before ColB, I didn't
relise how much harm drugs really did
to my brain, its been over 3 months now
since have had any stimulants and for the
first time in over a year my mind feels
clear and my brain seems to be healing
but still so much I cant remember, lots
of blanks. I wish I could go back in
time to September ColB which was the
first time I ever tried real drugs
when a friend Jake gave my ex Daz
a bag of meth to try with me, now I
wish I didnt give into him, I just did
not want him to do it alone or with some
strange guy as thought by doing it together
it would be safer it was a lot of fun

A0261PL
PaRT
4-1-35

HMP
Belmarsh

at first I admite that but after six
months on the effects were less so we
started taking more and adding E to
make it stronger, it got to a point when
I only saw him when he wanted to come
round to aless on he would drive me to
the dealer. we would spend the weekends
getting high then he would drive back to
kept on the monday or Tues depending if we
had anything left. If I had known the
damage it would do to my brain I wouldn't
have ever been tempted to try it. I hope
when I leave here that I can get the
message out to stop anyone being tempted
into drugs. I now know how it destroys
lifes, even tho I was never on adict it
just became routine to do it with ole,
yes I only ever did it when they wanted
to tho with there contents he was auth-
tic not stoyped. not like down syndrome he
was more than capable of telling me
exactly what he wanted and he loved
sex and being high otherwise he wouldn't
of kept coming back to me again and
again. Anyway sorry, just as on these
as police useing the fact he had some
emotional problems saying I took ad
vantage of him which is so untrue I

③

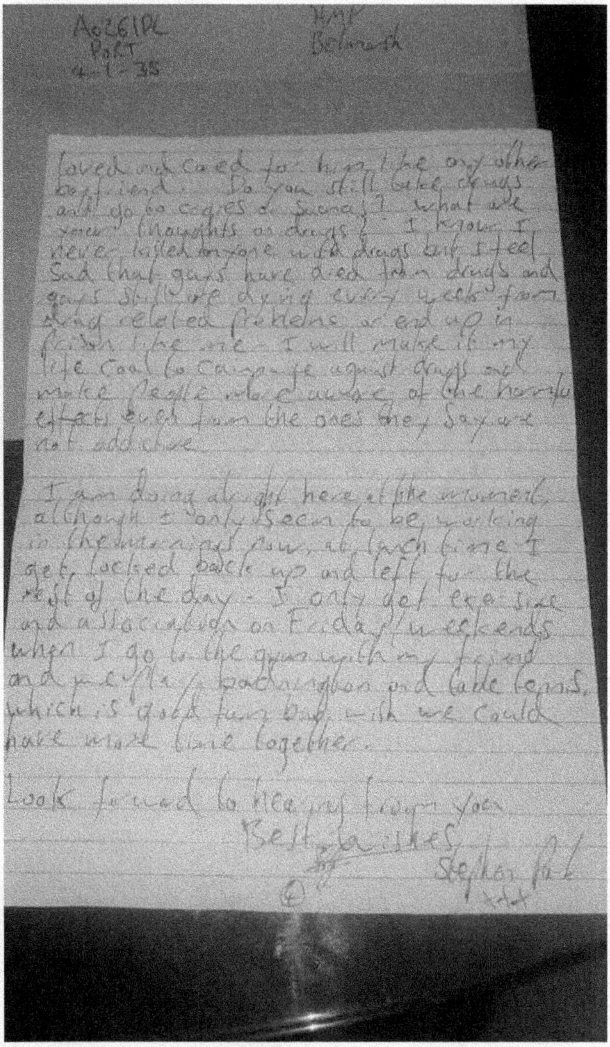

A0261PL
Port
4-1-35

HMP
Belmarsh

loved and cared for him like any other boyfriend. Do you still take drugs and go to orgies or saunas? What are your thoughts on drugs? I know I never killed anyone with drugs but I feel sad that guys have died from drugs and guys still are dying every week from drug related problems or end up in prison like me. I will make it my life goal to campaign against drugs and make people more aware of the harmful effects even from the ones they say are not addictive.

I am doing alright here at the moment, although I only seem to be working in the mornings now, at lunch time I get locked back up and left for the rest of the day. I only get exercise and association on Friday/weekends when I go to the gym with my friend and we play badminton and table tennis, which is good fun but wish we could have more time together.

Look forward to hearing from you

Best wishes,

Stephen Port
xxx

(4)

21

MARCH 24, 2016 LETTER

66 Dear Cody,

So nice to hear from you again. I thought you had given up on me. What did you do with your time in Ireland? I have never been, maybe you can take me with you next time? I am doing alright, and time goes by a bit quicker now that I have more things to do. I am still working in the ink shop, my friend in ink shop as well now, so it's nice to chat while working but he has lessons on a Tuesday. I have applied for lessons as well, but I got no response.

I get 11 pounds a week, which don't go far but buys a few biscuits.

My family and friends sent me some birthday money, so I bought a nice watch from the canteen and ordered a DVD player, radio, and a chessboard from Argos. Just I haven't got any CDs or DVDs to play. Would love to see the *Minions* movie and *Terminator Genisys*, and *Years and Years* on CD. Hint Hint!

I am still in a single cell, but my friend keeps his stuff in my cell as he's been having food stolen. He doesn't trust one of his cellmates. I am still going to the gym. I have put on more muscle and defined my six-pack better now, and gone back to being 84 kilograms. My friend weighs 57 kilograms have started training him with lifting weights. He works to get stronger, and he's lifting 5 kilograms each arm now, so he's improving. We train for 45 minutes then we go play badminton, we are not very good, but we have a good laugh.

I have more energy now that I no longer take any stimulants, which used to make me feel tired all the time. There's been no movement with my case. Still waiting for the CPS to send their final evidence, which is a three-week slate. My solicitor believes that they can't decide what to charge me with as it's now obviously clear that the guys died from a mixture of drugs and not just from GHB, and this proves that rape was not the intention otherwise, they would have only had GHB in their system and not meph etc. Also, as meph keeps you awake for hours and GHB would only add to the high but wouldn't knock you out, and you can't force someone to snort it.

It's clear there was content, so the murder charges should be dropped, and as I didn't administer the drugs, it's not manslaughter either. Also, they had poppers in their system, and as you know, you can only sniff this yourself, and you only take during sex. It proves they weren't being raped, and when they drug tested me, I had GHB in my system, so I didn't use it to rape unless I can rape myself.

Anyway, my plea hearing is next month, and the trial is October if it even goes to trial. Am not really missing sex, trying not to think about it. I just draw pictures of my last boyfriend, which helps ease the tension, but I do miss the kissing and cuddling and waking up in the mornings with the boyfriend next to me and his smile and watching movies together and going bowling together etc.

My family are alright but mum been a bit unwell. I phone her on Sunday morning this cheers her up a lot. My sister has started visiting me now once a month, and she brings me new clothes. I have to arrange a clothes exchange for her next visit as I am at my limit of what I am allowed. When she visits, she buys me a lot of chocolate from the visitors' canteen, had two dairy milk, a Cadbury cream egg, and a Twix with a couple of coffees.

It's nice to know what is going on out there. She says my ex-partner is doing alright but suffering a bit with his depression as all this has been a lot for him to take in. I can't wait till this nightmare is over, and I can get back to a normal life (without drugs). I would still love to come and stay with you but depends on what restrictions they put on me. Possibly won't be allowed to use my social sites again, which is fine with me. I have had a few letters from close friends, and my friend Mike has now been cleared to visit me, so he's just waiting to book a date now.

Do you go out on the scene much? Anyway, I look forward to hearing from you again soon. Please give my regards to you mum.

All the best,
love from
Stephen XXX."

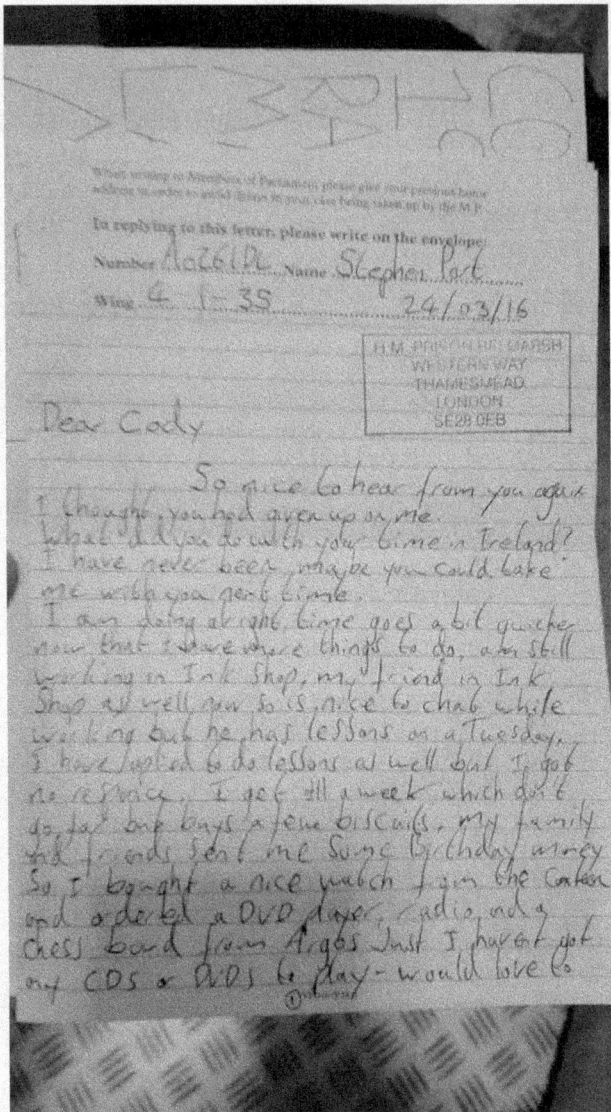

What writing to Members of Parliament please give your previous home address in order to avoid letters to your case being taken up by the M.P.

In replying to this letter, please write on the envelope:

Number A0261PL Name Stephen Port

Wing 4 1 35   24/03/16

H.M. PRISON BELMARSH
WESTERN WAY
THAMESMEAD
LONDON
SE28 0EB

Dear Cody

So nice to hear from you again. I thought you had given up on me. What did you do with your time in Ireland? I have never been, maybe you could take me with you next time.

I am doing alright, time goes a bit quicker now that I have more things to do, am still working in Ink Shop, my friend is Ink Shop as well now so is nice to chat while working but he has lessons on a Tuesday. I have applied to do lessons as well but I got no response. I get £11 a week which don't go far but buys a few biscuits. My family and friends sent me some birthday money so I bought a nice watch from the canteen and ordered a DVD player, radio, and a chess board from Argos but I haven't got any CDs or DVDs to play - would love to

See the Minions movie and Terminator
Genisys, and Years & Years on CD think that I
I am still in single cell but my friend
keeps his stuff in my cell as his been
having his food stolen, he doesn't trust one
of his cell mates.
I am still going to the gym, I have put on
more muscle and defined my six pack
better now and gone back to being 84kg
my friend who is 57kg have started training
him with lifting whith, he wants to get
stronger, his lifting 5kg each arm now so his
improving we train for 45min then we
go play badminton, we are not very good at
it but we have a laugh. I have more
energy now that I no longer take my slim-
plants which used to make me feel bloated all
the time.
There been no movement with my case,
still waiting for the CPS to send those
final evidence which is 3 weeks late,
my solicitor believes that they can't
decide what to charge me with as its
now obviously clear that the guys died
from a mixture of drugs and not just
from GHB and this proves that rape was
not the intention otherwise they would of
only had GHB in there system and not
②

meph etc also as meph keeps you awake
for hours and GHB would only add to
the high but wouldnt knock you out and
you cant make someone to snort it so
its clear there was content so the murder
charges should be dropped and as I didnt
administer the drugs its not manslaughter
either — also they had poppers n systemwork
as you know you can only sniff this
yourself and you only take during sex it
proves they wasnt being raped and when
they drug tested me I had GHB in my system
so thows I dont use it to rape unless I can
rape myself. Anyway my plea hearing
is next month and trial in October if
it ever goes to trial. Am not really missing sex, trying not to think about it, I just
draw pictures of my last of which helps
ease the tension but I do miss the kissing and cuddling and waking up in the
mornings with the Bf next to me and his
smile and watching movies together and
going bowling together etc.
My family are alright but Mum's been
a bit unwell. I phone her on a sunday
morning this cheers her up alot, my
sister has started visiting me now
once a month and she brings me new

clothes, i have to arrange a clothes exchange
for her next visit as than not my timing
of what am along, when she visits she
buys me lots of chocolate from the visitors
canteen, had 2 day milks, a cad cream
egg and a twix with couple of coffees,
is nice to know what is going on out there.
she says my partner is doing alright but
suffering a bit with his depression as
all this has been a lot for him to take in
I can't wait till this nightmare is over and
I can get back to a normal life (without
drugs) I would still love to come stay
with you but depends what restrictions
they put on me pos won't be aloud to use
my social sites again which is fine with
me. I have had a few letters from
close friends and my friend Mike has
now been cleared to visit me so his
just waiting to book a date now,
do you go out on the scene much?
Anyway, I look forward to hearing
from you again soon, please give my
regards to your Mum.

All the best
Love from
Stephen xxx

④

22

SEND MONEY PLEASE
LETTER

66 Dear Cody, sorry for my rushed letters of the weekend. I just wanted to let you know I received your letters and didn't want you to think I returned the items. I still don't know if they will let me have the *Star Wars Annual*. Well, fingers crossed they will let me. [Cody had sent the Star Wars annual to Port after the first letter].

I know I can receive magazines if sent direct from W.H. Smith [U.K. Bookstore chain] but not certain about other items from suppliers. I was told that you could call the prison to find out the numbers at the top of the page.

Not sure if they will allow me to have a watch or radio. I feel bad asking for cash, but if you could please post ten pounds, I can buy a pen, biscuits, order a magazine as hunger and boredom is getting me down. I will ask my dad to post the money back to you as soon as the bank will allow him access to my account.

I had asked the Governor [Prison Warden] to write to my bank to give my dad full permission to access my bank account. He will have to cancel my direct debits like phone and internet, that will probably take a few weeks.

How was your weekend? What did you do? I hope I will be able to lessons or work soon so I can at least have some money on my canteen and get off the wing, as I'm feeling really, really depressed at the moment. I'm just so glad I have you to write to, and I look forward to your reply.

I have a good legal team, and my QC is one of the best in the country. He's amazing, and he's confident he can prove my innocents. I have told my parents not to speak to the press after all the lies after they twisted everything to make it look certain I did it when there's only evidence to link me to two of them. Which I mentioned before, but I would never harm anyone. I would sooner kill myself than take another's life.

I've been watching *Big Bang Theory*, and glad there's new episodes on Thursday nights as seen all the repeats over and over. I don't follow my soaps but started to watch *Neighbors* and *Home & Away* here. I also watch *Star Gate* and *Star Trek* when it's on. I can't wait for the new *Top Gear* when Chris Evans takes over, but it won't be the same without Clarkson. But I love supercars, so I'll be happy if I can get to see something like the new Aston Martin DB10 that's in the new Bond movie. Wished I could see that.

Hopefully, I will be out of here when the DVD comes out. So much more I want to write, but I have to give this pen back to the insider as it's dinner time now and will get locked up after. I will post this on the way. All the best.

Stephen Port"

23

GETTING TO KNOW YOU LETTER

"Dear Cody, thank you so much for the money. I finally bought a pen and paper from the canteen. So, I can now write you many more letters. This is just a brief letter to let you know I received the money so that you don't have to worry.

I will write a longer letter today and try and answer as many of your questions as I can. I have to write on your letters a number next to your questions 1,2, 3 etc., so I can look back and remember what you asked as I tend to ramble on and forget what you asked, LOL.

They won't let me have the *Star*

Wars Annual until I leave. So, I have asked my solicitor to write to the Governor, so I have not shown any aggression towards anyone, and I have no history of violence of any kind. So, they have no reason not to give me the *Star Wars* book. But luckily, I got a *Star Wars* book from the library which had big print as I can see it as I have not got my glasses yet. Just there's no pictures in the book, though. I can now order a Saturday Sunday newspaper thanks to your money, so I can have a TV guide, they sometimes have a magazine with it.

I won't yet order a *Top Gear* magazine as I need the money to last, as I've spent 14 pounds already. I bought toothpaste and imperial leather soap as the prison stuff is crap. I got some coffee, digestives, caustic caramels, chocolate spread, porridge and some Jaffa cakes, which is not nice I ate them all at once, the whole packet on Saturday night while watching *Doctor Who*.

I have been watching *I'm a celebrity get me out of here*. I like George [George Shelley is a boy-band pop music singer in the UK], and I'm certain that he will most likely win. Not just because he's cute, but he seems to be able to do any of the challenges that he's faced with.

I would love to come stay with you in Manchester when I get out of here. Are you certain that would be okay? It's likely I will be allowed back to Barking, for my own safety, after what was said in the press. But I think I will sell the flat before I am released. Anyway, my friend Mike can take care of removing and storing my things, but I'm not allowed to contact him for three months. My sister is in contact with him, though and says he's doing alright and living back with his family until he's allowed back to my flat.

He's been a good friend to me, we first met ten years ago when I was an escort. He was a client, and we became really close as friends, not boyfriends, as he was married with three kids. He helped me when I was in prison back in March. He looked after my flat and checked the post, and paid the bills so that I still had a flat when I got released on an HDC tag.

[You have probably noticed that Port contradicts himself by in one letter saying that he owned his flat and would sell it before he gets out, while in another letter, his friend pays his bills for the flat as if he rents it].

He's going through a divorce, so I let him move into the flat as he wasn't happy in the family home. It helped me, and it helped him. He gets on really well with my family, and he became like a dad to my boyfriend, he didn't have parents as they disowned him for being gay, and he has autism. He used to help him with his college work and cook him dinner when I was at work when I was doing a late shift. That was a few years ago, though.

He got a job as a steward on the cruise liner, and he's doing really well now, the ex-boyfriend, not Mike.

Being an escort is really dangerous. It's vital you never accept a drink from a client. Always take your own drink, take money first, and be alert. I had a friend who was also an escort, and we would tell each other to where we were going and always gave the client's name and address or room number if it was a hotel. I would text him every hour to update him. He used to take some methadone before he went so that it made being with older men all the more bearable. But I preferred not to as I just wanted to get it done with, get paid and go home.

I never saw it as pleasure, just work which helped me save up a deposit for my flat. I only got into doing it when my friend said you're a good-looking lad with a nice body. Why not make some money from it, and he told me what he did? At first, I was a bit nervous about having sex with all the guys for money. But it wasn't that bad. Most of the clients I had just wanted some company or to just touched me. Some had the odd fetish and just wanted to dress me up in uniforms and take pictures of me etc. Some just paid me to go out for dinner with them. Would I be able to get a job on the doors or bar work in Manchester? As I want to get back into work as soon as possible when I am released.

To answer what I miss, I miss my home, my family, and friends. Good food, DVDs, toys [Not sex toys; Port actually liked to play with kid's toys], a comfortable sofa, going shopping and drinking, driving, and my last boyfriend and his beautiful smile, the way he kissed me and would rest his head on my shoulder and kiss my neck. He had an amazing blue eyes and short ginger hair. He loved Minions, and I used to buy him the toys. For his 23rd birthday, I bought him a massive cuddly "King Bob" from the movie. I liked them a lot as they are so funny. I love the humor.

Are you dating anyone at the moment? I only started using Grindr when a friend and dealer had offered me free bags of methadone if I found him guys for his parties and to use my pictures etc., and I did a few times. And I never stayed long at his parties as he was into some heavy stuff I didn't get involved with.

I have a varying taste in music. I like the one by Nightwish, Adele, Will Young. I wished I could get his new album called "Joy." I heard it on CFL Friday's show.

Next letter to follow, all the best.
Stephen Port"

PART V

B-SIDE AND RARETIES

24

POLICE MISCONDUCT

B *BC One* broadcast a documentary in March 2017 that suggested a catalog of police failings in the Metropolitan police's response to the deaths in this case. Crucial witnesses, such as Port's neighbor, who claimed Port would show up at his house with a large amount of a white powdery substance and liquor bottles, were not questioned. That neighbor claimed he received weird text messages from Port about Gabriel Kovari.

After Gabriel Kovari was found dead, his previous roommate, John Pape, searched the internet and was surprised to find several other unexplained overdose deaths in the Barking area. Pape found it strange that the Barking Dagenham Police did not link the cases. Pape found that peculiar, especially in the Anthony Walgate case, because their bodies were found in the exact location. The cases also had many similarities to the Kovari case.

It wasn't until Daniel Whitworth was found dead in the same park that John Pape called the police and demanded to know if the police thought the cases were connected and could be the results of murder. Pape was also very concerned for his safety, but the police told him not only were the cases not linked, but there was no killer out on the loose. So not to worry.

John Pape offered to come into the station to be interviewed by the police if he had some relevant information about Kovari's death. He knew about all the places and things that Kovari had done before his death, but the police showed no interest.

The neighborhood's widespread belief was that the police had no idea what they were doing in not connecting the two cases. The dog walker who found the two bodies in the park, Barbara Denham, couldn't understand why they wouldn't link the two murders. Even the local gay organization, the *Pink News*, reported a serial killer in the area and to be aware.

On Friday, May 12, 2017, the seventeen family members of the victims of Stephen Port filed a lawsuit against Scotland Yard, claiming that the officers discriminated against their relatives because they were gay. The High Court action was over "breaches of duty and inaction" and accused the police of breaching the Equality Act 2010. The families also claimed that the police were negligent and misused or abused their power by failing to investigate properly. Court documents revealed that they sought "aggravated and exemplary damages" over £200,000. The detectives admitted to missing the opportunity of spotting similarities between the killings.

The misconduct started when Port was jailed for perverting the course of justice in the death of Anthony Walgate, which ended up being his first victim. He was only given an eight-month sentence. Port claimed that Walgate overdosed in his flat and that he panicked and left the body out front of his apartment in June 2014. But then Port went on to kill three others after his release in September 2015. The families of the murdered men say they are insulted and distressed over the lack of police answers about the mistakes they made and wonder why Port was not caught sooner. Some seventeen officers faced misconduct probes after the case was referred to the Independent Police Complaints Commission.

The police admitted to catching Port due to missed opportunities, leaving the families with new hope that there was an end in sight. The

Commission compiled over 7000 pages of material on the cases and has completed its first draft.

During Port's trial, we discovered that he became obsessed with pornography that focused on both men and women being raped while they were out of control on drugs. Port went to dating websites or apps to meet his victims. It wasn't until after Port's trial that the police introduced new guidance to deal with allegations involving "Chemsex" incidents. And now, they must review 58 cases where people died from GHB poisoning in London during the years that Port was active in the community. The police are unaware of the total number of victims since Port also drugged and raped seven other victims in separate incidents, where the victims didn't die.

Mandy Pearson, Daniel Whitworth's stepmother, said, "We continue to seek answers and accountability from the police about how, for a whole year, they let us believe that Daniel had committed suicide, in which time Port went on to kill again. We hoped that the police would be held to account for their activities with Port now behind bars. It won't bring any of the boys back, but we've been determined to get to the bottom of what happened, so we hope this will help with that. We won't rest until we get the truth."

In January of 2021, a formal inquest was held

into the police conduct during the deaths of the four men. The final verdict was reached, saying that the police failings probably contributed to the ends of the victims. They also found that the local police did not conduct a background check on Port, leading to omissions and failures during the Walgate investigation.

Even though police claimed that the lack of resources caused their failings, the victim's families all claimed that it was prejudice because the victims were gay. Assistant Commissioner Helen Ball would formally apologize to the victim's families on behalf of the metropolitan police but claimed that the police were not homophobic.

25

LAWSUITS

The families of the four men raped and murdered by serial killer Stephen Port are now suing Scotland Yard for more than 200,000 GBP. Claiming the police failed them because the victims were gay. Despite the striking similarities between the killings, the police failed to link them until the family of Port's fourth victim, Jack Taylor, forced the proper investigation of Jack's death and the other three. Jack's two sisters claimed that their concerns over the initial investigation went unheeded because Jack had been dismissed as a gay and druggie, and that was it.

The papers were filed on May 12, 2017, by the seventeen surviving family members of the victims, stating that the police breached their

202 | GRINDR SERIAL KILLER

duties by inaction. They claim aggravated and exemplary damages from the police force because it violated the Equality Act 2010 by discriminating against the victims. After all, they were gay.

Three of the claims state that "The Claimant's" estimate of the value of damages based on the current evidence is 50,000 GBP. Jack Taylor's family is suing for 60,000 GBP. Jack's sisters, Donna and Jenny Taylor said, "The police should be held accountable for Jack's death. If they had done their job, Jack would still be here."

Immediately after these filings were made in court, the Metro Police issued their officers a toolkit and checklist to guide how to respond to allegations involving so-called chemsex or party and play incidents.

A Scotland Yard spokeswoman said, "We are aware of a civil lawsuit action lodged in the High Court in connection with the Stephen Port case. It would be inappropriate to comment further at this stage."

Scotland Yard retired detective Colin Sutton commented on the police department's handling of the case and failure to link the killings for the *BBC* in November 2018. "I'm baffled, to be honest. I can't explain how this could happen. Ultimately, all this stems from the fact that nobody recognized that these four very similar deaths of young gay men in a minimal area were linked.

They were treated as individual unexplained deaths rather than somebody looking at the bigger picture and the fact that they formed a series of murders all by one man. You've now got four deaths in the small area, and of course, the connection's not that difficult to make because you've got a name, you've got Stephen Port, who you know has told lies about the very first one."

A forensic psychologist Kerry Daynes, an advisor to the Home Office and the Prison Service, commented, "I think the police failure, in this case, is catastrophic. Drug-assisted sexual crime happens to members of all different communities. Just because you're a member of the gay community doesn't mean that you should be taken any less seriously than anybody else."

26

FOOD FOR THOUGHT

O ften, after a serial killer gets caught and the news spreads worldwide, people come forward and talk about their experiences or how they knew the killer. Stephen Port's case was no different.

Over time, several men had talked to different media outlets to tell their stories of how they knew Port and what had happened to them when they were with him. Of course, there are always those just seeking attention and creating complete falsehoods about knowing the killer for an unknown reason. But after sifting through these cases, I have only found two that have some proof to substantiate their contact with Port.

One was that of Fabio Porchat, now 28, who had a relationship with Port back in 2012 when he was 19. He had newly moved from Brazil to London, where he got a job as a waiter. While he was working one night, he met Port. The two of them hit it off and began dating. Porchat eventually moved in with Port at his Barking apartment. They stayed together for about one month. After they broke up, Porchat returned to Brazil and continued his life. Sometime in 2019, he read about a man in London named Stephen Port who was a serial killer. He was surprised and excited because he thought his one-time boyfriend had made a movie or documentary about a serial killer. Needless to say, he was shocked to find out that it was indeed a documentary about Stephen Port being a serial killer.

TIMELINE OF EVENTS

June 4, 2014: Barking Police were called about Stephen Port when he was seen walking with another man who seemed to be drugged and being led by Port back to his place. Police did not arrest Port even though they knew he had been taking illegal drugs.

❖

June 19, 2014: Police were called to Cooke Street to check on a man who seemed to have passed out on the street in front of an apartment building. It turned out that the apartment was where Stephen Port lived, and Port was also the person who called the police. Port initially told police that he didn't know who the man was, but they would later discover the two of them had been together earlier that evening. The dead man was later identified as **Anthony Walgate**, and Port hired him as an escort for the night, which led to Port's arrest.

❖

August 28, 2014: A woman walking her dog in the park area of St. Margaret's Church found a dead body, later identified as **Gabriel Kovari**.

❖

September 20, 2014: The same dog walker would find a second dead body in the same place she had about one month before. This time the victim was **Daniel Whitworth**, and he had a suicide note in his hand. Later, it was discovered that Port had written the suicide note.

❖

March 23, 2015: Stephen Port was convicted of perverting the course of justice (lying to police during an investigation) in the death of Anthony Walgate. Port served eight months in jail and was released on parole wearing an electronic monitor on his leg.

❖

September 14, 2015: Another body was discovered in the same vicinity on the St. Margaret's Church grounds. He was identified as **Jack Taylor**.

❖

October 15, 2015: After one month of the investigation going nowhere, Taylor's two sisters found the CCTV showing Taylor with Stephen Port the same evening he was found dead. Port was arrested and charged with the murder of Taylor.

❖

November 2016: Stephen Port was found guilty and sentenced to life imprisonment for the murders of four men: Anthony Walgate, 23; Gabriel Kovari, 22; Daniel Whitworth, 21; and Jack Taylor, 25, using fatal doses of date rape drug GHB.

REFERENCES

1. https://www.wusa9.com/article/news/local/dc/911-calls-from-metro-smoke-incident/65-286546066
2. https://www.gisborneherald.co.nz/local-news/20151009/judge-goes-hard-on-domestic-violence/
3. Findlater, Chloe: "10 Faked Crime Scenes With Good, Bad, And Bizarre Motivations." *Listverse*. October 29, 2017. https://listverse.com/2017/10/29/10-faked-crime-scenes-with-good-bad-and-bizarre-motivations/
4. https://en.wikipedia.org/wiki/Stephen_Port
5. De Simone, Daniel: "The killer the police missed." *BBC News*. November 25, 2016. https://www.bbc.co.uk/news/resources/idt-d32c5bc9-aa42-49b8-b77c-b258ea2a9205
6. Davies, Caroline: "Inquest into Stephen Port murders to examine police competence." *The Guardian*. October 5, 2021. https://www.theguardian.com/uk-news/2021/oct/05/stephen-port-murders-inquest-police-competence
7. Duffy, Nick: "Alleged gay hook-up killer 'eluded police by planted drug bottles and fake suicide note on victims." *PinkNews*. October 7, 2016.

https://www.pinknews.co.uk/2016/10/07/
alleged-gay-hook-up-killer-eluded-police-by-
planted-drug-bottles-and-fake-suicide-note-on-
victims/

8. Leeson, Lucy: "'Please be careful on dating apps' - murdered Hull man's aunt makes this desperate warning." *Hull Daily Mail.* June 21, 2018. https://www.hulldailymail.co.uk/news/ hull-east-yorkshire-news/please-careful-dating-apps-murdered-1696933

9. De Simone, Daniel: "How did police miss Barking serial killer Stephen Port?" *BBC News.* November 24, 2016. https://www.bbc.com/ news/magazine-38045742

10. Hopkins, Stephen: "Owen Jones Spearheads Criticism Of Police Warning On Dating Apps In Wake Of Stephen Port Case." *Huffington Post.* November 24, 2016. https://www. huffingtonpost.co.uk/entry/owen-jones-hits-back-at-police-dating-app-warnings-over-serial-killer-stephen-port_uk_5836b205e4b0ddedcf5c1304

11. Fieldhouse, Simon: "Old Bailey Central Criminal Courts London." http:// simonfieldhouse.com/old-bailey-central-criminal-courts-london/

12. "Families of men killed by Serial Killer Stephen Port 'insulted and distressed' over lack of police answers." *The Telegraph.* December 26, 2017.

https://www.telegraph.co.uk/news/2017/12/
26/families-men-killed-serial-killer-stephen-
port-insulted-distressed/

13. Gordon, Naomi: "The Barking Murders stars
    Stephen Merchant as you've never seen him
    before." *Cosmopolitan*. March 26, 2019. https://
    www.cosmopolitan.com/uk/entertainment/
    a26943007/the-barking-murders-stephen-port-
    serial-killer-grindr-stephen-merchant/

14. Sanford, Daniel; De Simone, Daniel: "Stephen
    Port: Victims' families 'appalled' at police
    inquiry progress." *BBC News*. May 19, 2017.
    https://www.bbc.com/news/uk-39978661.amp

15. De Simone, Daniel: "Stephen Port victims'
    families say legal funding unfair." *BBC News*.
    September 5, 2018. https://www.bbc.com/
    news/uk-45407465

16. Pettifor, Tom: "Families of serial killer Stephen
    Port's victims sue police as cops 'failed loved
    ones because they were gay'." *Mirror*. May 12,
    2017. https://www.mirror.co.uk/news/uk-
    news/families-serial-killer-stephen-ports-
    10411533

17. Bastos, Márcio: "Em program de Fábio Porchat,
    jovem conta Como descobriu que ex era um
    serial killer" [In Fábio Porchat's show, a young
    man tells how he found out that his ex was a
    serial killer] 26 August 2020.

18. Mr. Justice Openshaw: "R v Stephen Port: Sentencing Remarks of Mr. Justice Openshaw" (PDF). 25 November 2016.

19. Kirk, Tristan: "Stephen Port murder trial: Gay chef murdered four men by injecting them with lethal doses of date rape drug." *London Evening Standard*. October 5, 2016. Retrieved November 25, 2016.

20. Williams, Richard: "Suspected serial killer Stephen Port appeared on Celebrity MasterChef." *The Independent*. October 21, 2015. https://www.independent.co.uk/news/uk/home-news/suspected-serial-killer-stephen-port-appeared-on-celebrity-masterchef-a6702636.html

21. Khan, Shehab: "Stephen Port: Grindr serial killer appeals against murder convictions of four men." *The Independent*. Friday, August 31, 2018. https://www.independent.co.uk/news/uk/crime/stephen-port-grindr-serial-killer-ghb-appeal-murders-convictions-a8516196.html

22. Osborne, Samuel: "Stephen Port: Police investigate 58 date rape deaths after 'Grindr Serial Killer' found guilty of the murder of four men." *The Independent*. Thursday, November 24, 2016. https://www.independent.co.uk/news/uk/crime/stephen-port-grindr-killer-met-police-date-rape-crimes-investigation-a7436161.html

23. Osborne, Samuel: "Stephen Port Guilty: Grindr Serial Killer to be sentenced for murder of four men." *The Independent*. November 23, 2016. https://www.independent.co.uk/news/uk/crime/stephen-port-guilty-verdict-court-grindr-serial-killer-murders-gay-men-latest-a7433486.html

24. London Scotland Yard: "Police interviews with GHB serial killer Stephen Port." June 2014.

25. Metropolitan Police Service: "A man has been charged with four counts of murder concerning the deaths of four men." October 15, 2015.

26. Evans, Martin: "Gay serial killer Stephen Port guilty of date rape drug murders of four young men." *The Telegraph*. November 23, 2016. https://www.telegraph.co.uk/news/2016/11/23/serial-killer-stephen-port-guilty-date-rape-drug-deaths-three/

27. Gayle, Damien; Davies, Caroline: "Alleged serial killer Stephen Port 'had the appetite for sex with unconscious men.'" *The Guardian*. October 5, 2016. https://www.theguardian.com/uk-news/2016/oct/05/alleged-serial-killer-had-appetite-for-sex-with-unconscious-men

28. "Stephen Port trial: Alleged serial killer 'tried to frame a victim." *BBC News*. October 6, 2016. https://www.bbc.com/news/uk-england-london-37573891

29. Wilford, Greg: "Stephen Port: Police missed Grindr serial killer because victims were gay, families say in the lawsuit" *The Independent*. June 3, 2017. https://www.independent.co.uk/news/uk/crime/grindr-stephen-port-scotland-yard-met-police-homophobia-serial-killer-a7734031.html

30. "What is chemsex and why does it matter?" *BMJ* 2015; 351 DOI: https://doi.org/10.1136/bmj.h5790 Published November 3, 2015.

ABOUT THE AUTHOR

Alan R Warren is a Bestselling Author, the Producer, and lead host of the popular NBC Radioshow House of Mystery and Inside Writing, both heard on the 106.5 F.M. Los Angeles/102.3 F.M. Riverside/ 1050 A.M. Palm Springs/ 540 A.M. KYAH Salt Lake City/ 1150 A.M. KKNW Seattle/Tacoma and Phoenix.

His bestselling true crime books in Canada include *Beyond Suspicion: The True Story of Colonel Russell Williams*, which will be featured on CNN's *Lies, Crimes, & Videos* (Season 4), and *Murder Times Six: The True Story of the Wells Gray Park Murders*. In America, his bestsellers include *The Killing Game: Serial Killer Rodney Alcala*, which was featured on several television shows such as *Very Scary People*

with Donny Walberg, Oxygen's *Mark of a Killer*, Reelz' *Killer Trophies*, and soon to be included in a four-part Sundance Channel documentary called *Death's Date*. His bestseller, *Doomsday Cults: The Devil's Hostages*, was featured on Vice's *Dark Side of the '90s*.

His latest series, *Killer Queens*, is a six-part book series covering murders that affect the Gay Community. So far, it includes Book 1 - Leopold & Loeb, Book 2 - Butcher of Hanover: Fritz Haarmann, Book 3 - Grindr Serial Killer: Stephen Port, and Book 4 - Bruce McArthur: Toronto Gay Killer.

ALSO BY ALAN R. WARREN

Killer Queens is a new series of historical fiction books based on true stories. Sources, such as police reports and newspaper articles, are examined to gather as many facts as possible surrounding each case. As with any work of fiction, some creative additions are made when telling these stories, usually within the conversations between the personalities involved. The various sources are the basis of these conversations and hopefully, make them come alive for the readers to help understand what was meant by those words.

LEOPOLD & LOEB: THE MURDER OF BOBBY FRANKS (KILLER QUEENS 1)

Book 1 of the series focuses on what has been called "The Crime of the Century" in 1920s United States. At the center of this murder case were Nathan Leopold Jr. and Richard Loeb – two wealthy University of Chicago students who, in May of 1924, kidnapped and murdered 14-year-old Bobby Franks.

With Leopold and Loeb, both

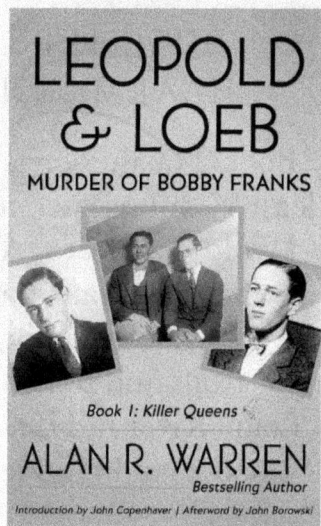

males, the dominance shifted from one to the other. Regardless of who held it, the result was the same. They were both very interested in crime and pushing the envelope for the next thrill. The vicious "thrill kill" of Bobby Franks was the bloody result of an intense and unhealthy co-dependent bond between the murdering duo.

As you read the exploration of the case in this book, ask yourself: Would these young men be as vulnerable to their manipulations today? If they couldn't have harnessed and used shame as a control tactic, would they have been as successful at recruiting a criminal counterpart? Finally, to what degree can we hold the prevalent homophobia of this era accountable as a force to bear on this tragedy?

BUTCHER OF HANOVER: FRITZ HAARMANN (KILLER QUEENS 2)

Book 2 of the series focuses on the serial killer of at least 27 young men and boys in Germany in the post-World War 1 era. At the center of this murder case were Fritz Haarmann and Hans Grans, who were lovers while committing these murders. It wasn't until the skulls and bones started washing ashore from the Leine River in Hanover that Germany realized they had a cold-blooded serial killer in their country.

Unlike Leopold and Loeb murder case covered in Book

BUTCHER of HANOVER

FRITZ HAARMANN

Book 2: Killer Queens

ALAN R. WARREN
Bestselling Author

Foreword by Mike Browne

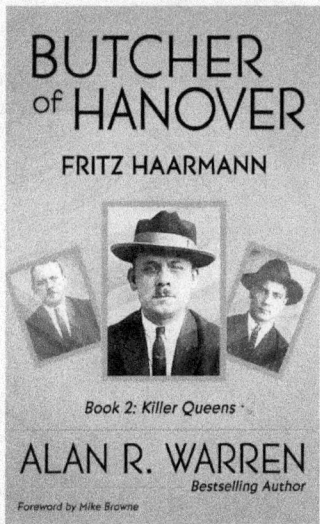

1, where the dominance shifted from one to the other, Fritz Haarmann was the dominant partner in this case. He carried out each of the murders and dismemberment of the bodies himself, even though he claimed that Grans chose who was to be murdered in court.

As you read the exploration of the case in this book, ask yourself, did Haarmann murder each victim to keep his lover Hans Grans to stay with him? Did Grans decide who it was that was to be murdered? The evidence on this case will keep you on the edge of your seat, trying to determine who was really behind these gruesome murders.

MURDER TIMES SIX: THE TRUE STORY OF THE WELLS PARK MURDERS

"The author even had me (who conducted the interview) on the edge of my seat as I was turning the pages as "the Detective" was trying to unearth the unspeakable truth."

— *SGT. MIKE EASTHAM R.C.M.P.*

It was a crime unlike anything seen in British Columbia. The horror of the "Wells Gray Murders" almost forty years ago transcends decades.

On August 2, 1982, three generations of a family set out on a camping trip – Bob and Jackie Johnson, their two daughters, Janet, 13 and Karen, 11, and Jackie's parents, George and Edith Bentley. A month later, the Johnson family car was found off a mountainside logging road near Wells Gray Park completely burned out. In the back seat were the incinerated remains of four adults, and in the trunk were the two girls.

But this was not just your average mass murder. It was much worse. Over time, some brutal details were revealed; however, most are still only known to the murderer, David Ennis (formerly Shearing). His crimes had far-reaching impacts on the family, community, and country. It still does today. Every time Shearing attempts freedom from the parole board, the grief is triggered as everyone is forced to relive the horrors once again.

Murder Times Six shines a spotlight on the crime that captured the attention of a nation, recounts the narrative of a complex police investigation, and

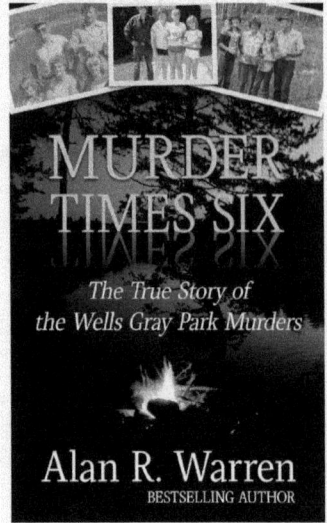

discusses whether a convicted mass murderer should ever be allowed to leave the confines of an institution. Most importantly, it tells the story of one family forever changed.

JFK ASSASSINATION: THE HOUSE OF MYSTERY INTERVIEWS - VOLUME II

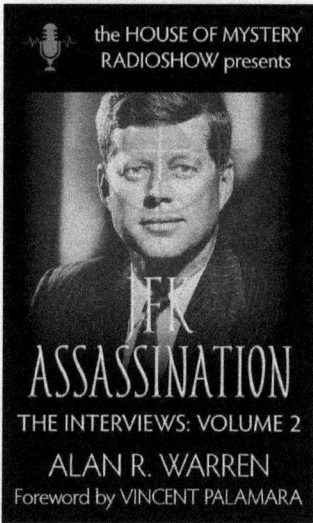

the HOUSE OF MYSTERY
RADIOSHOW presents

JFK
ASSASSINATION
THE INTERVIEWS: VOLUME 2
ALAN R. WARREN
Foreword by VINCENT PALAMARA

The House of Mystery Radio Show has been on the air for ten years, broadcasting in over a dozen cities in the U.S. It started as a way to interview guests knowledgeable in many of the world's mysteries involving crime, science, religion, history, paranormal, conspiracies, etc. The House of Mystery Interview series is a curated collection of interviews from the show. Each volume focuses on one of the mysteries, providing the background and reproducing the main points discussed in the interviews. There will be no committed answer at the end, as the Interviews series does not attempt to solve the case. Instead, it provides the most compelling aspects of each theory held by different experts. This series is an excellent reference for researchers and a good overview for those unfamiliar with the case. Online links to the actual interviews are included.

Volume 2 of the Interview Series, "JFK Assassination," covers the unrivaled historical mystery of historical mysteries. The JFK assassination is the grandfather of all conspiracies in America and arguably where they all started. A highly popular President with movie star looks and charisma, effecting significant changes in society, was brutally cut down in his prime. The official story was that JFK was killed by a sole assassin, Lee Harvey Oswald. However, many conspiracy theorists believe in an assassination plot involving the FBI, CIA, U.S. military, VP LBJ, Cuba's Fidel Castro, Russia's KGB, the Mafia, or some combination of those entities.

The research and interviewing of the JFK assassination experts lasted for over six years. Arguments and counter-arguments from a diverse mix of bestselling authors make for some interesting discussions. And some of the authors interviewed are considered just as controversial as the mystery itself. Most authors focused on who they believe was responsible for the assassination. Others narrowed their focus on certain related aspects, such as the Zapruder film, Nix film, Garrison Tapes, etc. All information collected from each expert adds value to the overall mystery.

IN CHAINS: THE DANGEROUS WORLD OF HUMAN TRAFFICKING

Human trafficking is the trade of people for forced labor or sex. It also includes the illegal extraction of human organs and tissues. And it is an extremely ruthless and dangerous industry plaguing our world today.

IN CHAINS

THE DANGEROUS WORLD OF HUMAN TRAFFICKING

BESTSELLING AUTHOR
ALAN R WARREN

Most believe human trafficking occurs in countries with no human rights legislation. This is a myth. All types of human trafficking are alive and well in most of the developed countries of the world like the United States, Canada, and the UK. It is estimated that $150 billion a year is generated in the forced labor industry alone. It is also believed that 21 million people are trapped in modern day slavery – exploited for sex, labor, or organs.

Most also believe since they live in a free country, there is built-in protection against such illegal practices. But for many, this is not the case. Traffickers tend to focus on the most vulnerable in our society, but trafficking can happen to anyone. You will see how easy it can happen in the stories included in *In Chains*.

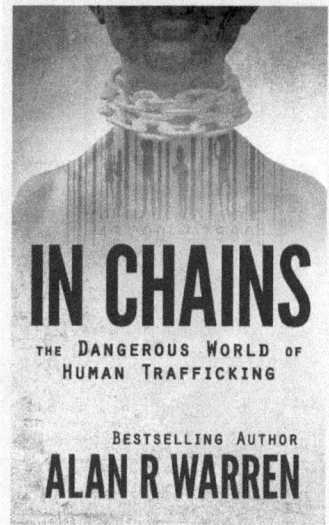

www.ingramcontent.com/pod-product-compliance
Lightning Source LLC
Chambersburg PA
CBHW062126020426
42335CB00013B/1113